For Josiah Bunting,
Fellow Admirer of Lincoln
Cullom Davis
November 27, 1989

Edited by
Cullom Davis
Charles B. Strozier
Rebecca Monroe Veach
and Geoffrey C. Ward

The Public and the Private

LINCOLN

Contemporary Perspectives

SOUTHERN ILLINOIS UNIVERSITY PRESS
Carbondale and Edwardsville

FEFFER & SIMONS, INC. London and Amsterdam

Grateful acknowledgment is made for permission to quote from *The Collected Works of Abraham Lincoln*, edited by Roy P. Basler. Copyright 1953 by The Abraham Lincoln Association. Reprinted by permission of Rutgers University Press.

Chapter one is from a biography of Abraham Lincoln by Charles B. Strozier, to be published by Basic Books, Inc., Publishers, New York, in 1980.

Library of Congress Cataloging in Publication Data

Main entry under title:

The Public and the private Lincoln.

   Includes bibliographical references and index.
   1. Lincoln, Abraham, Pres. U.S., 1809–65—Addresses, essays, lectures. 2. Presidents—United States—Biography—Addresses, essays, lectures.
I. Davis, Cullom, 1935–
E457.8.P97   973.7′092′4 [B]   79-9803
ISBN 0-8093-0921-1

Contents

CONTENTS

Preface

Each generation of Americans must come to terms with the commanding figure of Abraham Lincoln. Not only has Lincoln become a man for all seasons, parties, and causes, but his life and example seem to speak with pointed clarity to the needs and issues of each era. The Lincoln ideal offers national unity in times of discord, political acumen in periods of stalemate, compassion and justice in an age of oppression, and vision in times of doubt.

The Lincoln Sesquicentennial and Civil War Centennial were occasions for accelerated study, but their passing has diminished neither the interest in Lincoln nor the importance of fresh Lincoln scholarship. Scholars as well as the general public must confront Lincoln, and they do so by rediscovering and reassessing him in the context of their own times. One generation's research methodology, interpretive bent, or climate of opinion stimulates interest in new topics and new issues.

The Public and the Private Lincoln: Contemporary Perspectives combines timely themes with the timeless figure of Lincoln. Nine original essays by recognized scholars of Lincoln and nineteenth-century America examine the public and the private Lincoln anew, interpreting him from a contemporary perspective. While each essay stands on its own, collectively they focus on three themes of both transcendent and current interest: "The Private Lincoln," "Lincoln and the Idea of Progress," and "Lincoln, Politics and War."

Lincoln's private and family life and his personal relations with other people are a subject that has been the victim of both neglect and mythology. Modern research approaches in psychohistory and contemporary interests in women's history and minority groups offer a healthy antidote. In "The Private Lincoln" Charles Strozier, Kathryn Kish Sklar, and Roy P. Basler suggest a significant linkage between Lincoln's searches for sexual and professional identity, a new dimension in the mutual understanding between Lincoln and his wife Mary Todd, and some contrasts between Lincoln's public and personal dealings with blacks and women.

In this age of controversy over material growth, technology and modernization it is instructive to examine Lincoln's views on economic development and social order. Both G. S. Boritt and Norman Graebner concentrate on the largely unexplored subject of economic development, but from the separate standpoints, respectively, of the individual and the nation. George M. Fredrickson traces Lincoln's evolving thought on the principal intellectual problem of the time: determining the proper limits for a militant and aggressive democracy.

Politics, the exercise of power in a constitutional democracy, and wartime presidential leadership are central issues of the American experience that have received heightened attention in recent years. The pivotal experience in Lincoln's political ascent was his 1858 contest with Stephen A. Douglas for the U.S. Senate. Christopher Breiseth sheds new light on that crucial campaign by examining the intense Springfield press rivalry over the two candidates. Don E. Fehrenbacher uses the Civil War experience to consider important and perennial questions about constitutional limits on the president in wartime. He concludes that Lincoln exercised restraint but nevertheless set fateful precedents in consolidating national power and strengthening the executive arm. Richard N. Current portrays Lincoln the war leader against the larger canvas of America's secular religion, our historic mission to serve as a model of successful democratic government.

Each of these nine studies contributes to a heightened understanding of Abraham Lincoln, and together they represent the best of current scholarship on the man, seasoned reflections by noted Lincoln scholars, and fresh ideas on the enduring and timely meaning of Lincoln as a symbol and historical figure.

The essays were selected and edited principally from papers delivered at a conference on "Lincoln's Thought and the Present" sponsored by Sangamon State University in Springfield, Illinois. The conference was funded with generous support from the National Endowment for the Humanities and the Illinois Bicentennial Commission, whose assistance is gratefully acknowledged.

Springfield, Illinois   The Editors
January, 1979

Notes on Contributors

Roy P. Basler, honorary consultant in American Studies, Library of Congress, is the editor of *The Collected Works of Abraham Lincoln* (1953–55, *Supplement*, 1974) and the author of *The Lincoln Legend* (1935) and *A Touchstone for Greatness* (1974).

Gabor S. Boritt, assistant professor of history at Memphis State University, is the author of *Lincoln and the Economics of the American Dream* (1978) and numerous articles on Lincoln. He has received various awards for his teaching, research, and writing—most recently a postdoctoral fellowship at Harvard University.

Christopher N. Breiseth, professor of history, Sangamon State University, is the author of "Lincoln and Frederick Douglass: Another Debate," *Journal of the Illinois State Historical Society* (1975). He is continuing his study of Lincoln, Stephen A. Douglas, and the issue of race in the Springfield of the late 1850s and early 1860s. Breiseth served from 1977 to 1979 as president of the Board of Directors of the Springfield (Illinois) Urban League.

Richard N. Current, University Distinguished Professor of History, University of North Carolina at Greensboro, is the author of *The Lincoln Nobody Knows* (1958). Among his numerous other publications: *Old Thad Stevens* (1942), *Three Carpetbag Governors* (1968), and *Wisconsin: A Bicentennial History* (1977).

Don E. Fehrenbacher, Coe Professor of History and American Studies, Stanford University, is the author of *Prelude to Greatness: Lincoln in the 1850's* (1962) and *The Dred Scott Case: Its Significance in American Law and Politics* (1978). He edited *Abraham Lincoln, A Documentary Portrait* (1964) and *The Leadership of Abraham Lincoln* (1970). He also completed and edited David M. Potter's *The Impending Crisis* (1976).

George M. Fredrickson, professor of history, Northwestern University, is the author of *The Inner Civil War: Northern Intellectuals and the Crisis of the Union* (1965), *The Black Image in the White Mind: The Debate on Afro-American Character and Destiny, 1817–1914* (1971), and "A Man but Not a Brother: Abraham Lincoln and Racial Equality," *Journal of Southern History* 41 (1975): 39–58.

Norman A. Graebner is Edward R. Stettinius Professor of Modern American History at the University of Virginia. Before moving to Virginia he taught at Iowa State University and the University of Illinois, Champaign-Urbana. He has written or edited sixteen books which include *Empire on the Pacific*, *The Enduring Lincoln*, *Ideas and Diplomacy*, *Cold War Diplomacy*, *Freedom in America*, and *The Age of Global Power*.

Kathryn Kish Sklar, associate professor of history, University of California at Los Angeles, is the author of *Catharine Beecher, A Study in Domesticity* (1973). She is on the editorial board of the *Journal of American History* and has published several articles on the history of women.

Charles B. Strozier, associate professor of history, Sangamon State University, and visiting assistant professor of psychiatry, Rush Medical College, Chicago, has published a number of articles on psychohistory and is the editor of the *Psychohistory Review*.

PART 1
The Private Lincoln

ONE

The Search for Identity and Love in Young Lincoln

CHARLES B. STROZIER

The study of Abraham Lincoln as a young man has been left largely to antiquarians and romanticizers. As a result, we are probably better informed about the trivial and more confused about the significant events of his formative years than about those of any other figure in American history. Most of us know—or think we know—a good deal more about his rail-splitting or his absentmindedness than we do about such central questions as why he had such difficulty choosing a career; what lay behind his awkward, torturous courting of Mary Owens and Mary Todd; and what produced his periodic, paralyzing bouts of depression and melancholy. In suggesting some tentative answers to these and related questions, I will draw upon a considerable body of documentary evidence on Lincoln before the mid-1840s. My approach throughout is avowedly psychohistorical; that is, I have attempted to apply concepts from psychoanalytic theory critically and intelligently to bring the evidence alive in new ways.

From 1831 to 1837 Lincoln lived in New Salem, Illinois, as a young man in his twenties. This small, bustling community with a buoyant sense of its own importance had been staked out as an entrepreneurial venture in 1829 to rival Cincinnati and St. Louis. There were many artisans and the community included two physicians, one a graduate of Dartmouth (John Allen), the loquacious Mentor Graham, and a slick businessman, William Greene. At its founding in 1829 New Salem had as much apparent urban potential as the larger town of Springfield (which had five hundred people in 1830). Men—and women—deliberately gathered in a debating society to discuss the range of human affairs within their horizons;[1] and the moody intellectual figure of Lincoln reading on a woodpile was thought unusual but not weird.[2] As it turned out New Salem failed economically, and in 1836 the post office was moved to Petersburg which also became the seat of the newly formed Menard County in 1839.[3]

Lincoln arrived in New Salem in July, 1831, having just taken a load of produce down the Mississippi to New Orleans on Denton Offutt's flatboat. It was some five months after he had left his home.[4] Lincoln's first job in the village was to clerk in Offutt's store, a job he carried out affably but without commitment. This job soon gave way to service in the Black Hawk War for which he volunteered on April 21, 1832, and was elected captain by his company. Lincoln found that honor a source of more satisfaction than any subsequent success in life.[5] When in May his term ended, he reenlisted for twenty more days in the service of Capt. Elijah Iles, and then in June he signed on for thirty more days in Jacob M. Early's company.[6] This extended service was not a result of military need; Lincoln himself later ridiculed his bloody encounters with mosquitos[7] and told William Herndon that the only reason he served so long was that he had no other work.[8]

So Lincoln drifted back to New Salem. He toyed with the idea of "learning the black-smith trade" and considered the study of law, but he "rather thought he could not succeed at" this "without a better education."[9] Even before his first arrival in the village, he had announced his intention to run for office. Shortly after his return from the war, in 1832, he sought election to the legislature. He lost the election, though he carried his own precinct—New Salem—by 277 to 7.[10] Surviving on odd jobs, he next stumbled onto the purchase of a store with William Berry. With the store he assumed a heavy mortgage and responsibilities. These he did not seem prepared to handle, and he got little help from Berry, who proceeded to drink himself to death. As Lincoln later commented, "Of course they [Lincoln and Berry] did nothing but get deeper and deeper in debt." In no time, "The store winked out."[11]

Lincoln also tried surveying during the New Salem period. John Calhoun, the county surveyor, had befriended him and recommended him as his assistant. As Lincoln described it: "He [Lincoln] accepted, procured a compass and chain, studied Flint, and Gibson a little, and went at it. This procured bread, and kept soul and body together."[12] In his attempt to master the necessary mathematics to do surveying, Lincoln had enlisted the help of Mentor Graham. As Benjamin P. Thomas writes: "Often he and Graham stayed awake until midnight, interrupting their calculations only when Mrs. Graham ordered them out for a fresh supply of wood for the fire." [13] But this new venture was almost as ill-fated as the investment in the store. In order to begin surveying, Lincoln had purchased on credit from William Watkins a horse, saddle, and bridle for $57.86. Lincoln failed to make the payments for these items, and on April 26, 1834, Watkins got a judgment in the Sangamon County Circuit Court on Lincoln's personal possessions. [14] Though a competent surveyor, [15] Lincoln was hardly dedicated enough to become a successful one.

Lincoln also served as village postmaster, a post to which he was appointed on May 7, 1833. Though a Whig, he received the post during the Jackson administration because, in his own words, "the office . . . [was] too insignificant, to make his politics an objection." [16] The mail arrived once each week. Postage was determined by the number of pages and the distance the letter traveled. Thus a single sheet cost six cents for the first thirty miles, ten cents for thirty to eighty miles, and so on. There were no stamps or envelopes. Letters were simply folded and sealed, and the postage charge, written in the upper right hand corner, was paid by the person receiving the letter. [17] Possibly, for Lincoln, the best part of being postmaster was the opportunity it gave him to read all the papers. [18] But during his tenure in office, which lasted until May 30, 1836, Lincoln was neither conscientious nor competent. On September 17, 1835, New Salem settler Matthew S. Marsh wrote his brother: "The Post Master is very careless about leaving his office open and unlocked during the day—half the time I go in and get my papers, etc., without anyone being there as was the case yesterday. The letter was only marked twenty-five [cents] and even if he had been there and known it was double, he would not have charged me any more." [19] Marsh may have been something of a busybody, but Lincoln also had trouble with George C. Spears, to whom he wrote on July 1, 1834: "At your request I send you a receipt for the postage on your paper. I am some what surprised at your request. I will however comply with it. The law requires News paper postage to be paid in advance and now that I have waited a full year you choose to wound my feelings by insinuating that unless you get a receipt I will probably make you pay it again." [20]

All these New Salem activities of Lincoln's were necessarily part-time affairs. And they were in turn supplemented by occasional work splitting rails, working at the mill, harvesting, and tending store for Samuel Hill. After December, 1834, Lincoln served as the local agent for the *Sangamo Journal* and regularly clerked at the polls on election days.[21] He even spent the better part of one winter working at Isaac Burner's still.[22] Between these diverse and not particularly demanding duties, he only gradually came to make creative use of his free time. He never read widely and until 1834 he was too intimidated by his lack of education to begin the study of law.[23] Even after John T. Stuart encouraged him to start reading law, he did it selectively, though carefully.[24] He had access to the law books of H. E. Dummer and Stuart and could have delved into Stuart's fine personal library.[25] The books were available, but he was not ready for them.

Only after joining the legislature did Lincoln achieve any consistent success. He was elected in 1834, 1836, 1838, and 1840. Even this service in the legislature was a part-time activity. Each regular session met from late November in the year of election until February or March of the next year. Frequently, there were special sessions, such as the one in the summer of 1837 to deal with the financial panic. Lincoln the legislator developed slowly. He gradually won respect from his colleagues in the ranks of the Whig minority, and in his last term he became minority leader. But he was only one of the many legislators instrumental in moving the state capital from Vandalia to Springfield in 1837. As a legislator, Lincoln was always diligent and earnest but not always wise and responsible. Paul Simon, who has thoroughly investigated Lincoln's legislative career, chastizes him for his ambiguous stand on education.[26] Simon is even more critical of Lincoln's unequivocal support of the Illinois Internal Improvement Act, which nearly ruined the financial position of Illinois by burdening the state with an overwhelming debt for the next four decades. The act began as a ridiculously optimistic venture to encourage economic development by a program of improvements costing ten and a quarter million dollars. Hardly any improvements were actually made and most of the funds ended up in speculators' pockets. By 1857 the debt stood at seventeen million dollars; not until 1882 were the bonds finally paid off. Simon concludes quite sensibly that Lincoln learned a great deal about the operation of government and politics during his years in the legislature.[27] This education, however, was costly; to provide it, the state almost went bankrupt.

Lincoln during the New Salem period was, in short, undirected and unfocused, charming and well liked by his neighbors, but singularly unsuccessful in most ventures he undertook. He had failed in a series of enterprises, which brought two law suits against him for failing to pay his personal debts. He fell into surveying as he did splitting rails or delivering the mail or working in the still—by chance, as opportunity beckoned and the need to survive demanded. Even in his most rewarding activity in these years, serving in the legislature, he felt his way cautiously and not without making some serious errors in judgment.

Yet drive and ambition sustained creative tensions for Lincoln in these years. His energies were diffused because they lacked the unifying purpose that a coherent identity provides and that he himself was eventually to achieve. Compare the young Lincoln of the mid-1830s with the mature Lincoln of a decade later. By the mid-1840s he was a successful lawyer in Springfield (earning on the average more than the governor of Illinois). He was tight with the money that was accumulating at a healthy pace. He was widely known and respected. And from 1846 to 1848 he served as a U.S. congressman who opposed the Mexican War because he was convinced his own country was the aggressor.

Lincoln's long, stumbling search for satisfying work with which to supplement his political career may in part have been simply a reflection of his lack of a formal education. But his experimentation may have also been part of a larger search for personal coherence and integrity, a search that theoretically makes sense in terms of psychoanalytic conceptualizations of identity. Sigmund Freud, as an old man, was asked what defines normality. He replied with the terseness characteristic of his old age: "Lieben und arbeiten" (to love and to work). Each person must discover for himself how to love and to work. That process of discovery may be labeled "the search for identity." Neither dimension of identity—the sexual or the professional—is necessarily causative or primary, but we do not expect disturbance in one area to be isolated from disturbance in the other. An inability to love precludes working that is free from compulsive fastidiousness; and the commitment to professional activity that realizes one's potential and risks failure flows from a core sense of sexual identity. It is during the stage of late adolescence and early adulthood, in Erik Erikson's formulation, that biological imperatives and social expectations force a lasting resolution of these issues.[28]

Lincoln's first documented relationship with a woman of his own age appears to have been with Mary Owens, "an amiable, attractive

Kentucky girl of considerable culture." [29] It was a curious affair, but the complicated way he dealt with her foreshadows his tortured courting of Mary Todd. Lincoln first met Mary in 1833 when she visited her sister, Mrs. Bennett Abell, in New Salem. Late in 1836 Mary returned to the village and Lincoln soon began to court her. There never appeared to be much passion on either side; nevertheless, by May, 1837, they were clearly discussing marriage. Yet Lincoln was circumspect and ambiguous in his marriage proposal to Mary in a letter dated May 7, 1837: "Whatever woman may cast her lot with mine, should any ever do so, it is my intention to do all in my power to make her happy and contented; and there is nothing I can immagine, that would make me more unhappy than to fail in the effort. I know I should be much happier with you than the way I am, provided I saw no signs of discontent in you. . . . What I have said I will most positively abide by, provided you wish it. My opinion is that you had better not do it." [30] In other words, Lincoln was saying, "I want what you want and I most of all want to avoid hurting you; if you really want me, I'll marry you; but since you probably don't maybe we shouldn't marry so you won't be hurt."

A little over three months later, Lincoln broke off his relationship with Mary, and did so in a confused fashion. He wrote: "I can not see you, or think of you, with entire indifference," a phrasing which cast his supposedly affectionate feeling into a double negative. He continued: "I want in all cases to do right, and most particularly so, in all cases with women." Doing right in this case, Lincoln suggested, probably meant leaving her alone. If that was her desire then he urged her simply not to answer the letter. Such a solution to their "romance" forced her to act and made Lincoln the passive recipient of her decision. He then made the same point again with greater emphasis: "Do not understand by this, that I wish to cut your acquaintance. I mean no such thing. What I do wish is, that our further acquaintance shall depend upon yourself. . . . If you feel yourself in any degree bound to me, I am now willing to release you, provided you wish it; while, on the other hand, I am willing, and even anxious to bind you faster, if I can be convinced that it will, in any considerable degree, add to your happiness." [31]

Lincoln, with apparent disregard for himself, desperately feared hurting Mary. At all costs he sought to make her happy, and if his actions hurt her he was hurt even more himself. He seemed to love ambivalently, and at the point of marriage with its potential of intimacy, he withdrew in a clumsy, if genuine, expression of sympathy for Mary's feelings. One of the difficulties we face in interpreting Lincoln's relationship with Mary Owens is that Lincoln himself described the love affair to Mrs. Orville Hickman Browning, the wife of a state senator from Quincy, as a far more casual event than my description would have it. Writing to Mrs. Browning on April 1, 1838, Lincoln recounted that he had first seen Mary in 1833 and had not been displeased; that in 1836 his friend, Mrs. Abell, had played matchmaker for a willing Lincoln; but that when he saw Mary he was aghast:

I knew she was over-size, but she now appeared a fair match for Falstaff; I knew she was called an "old maid", and I felt no doubt of the truth of at least half of the appelation; but now, when I beheld her, I could not for my life avoid thinking of my mother; and this, not from withered features, for her skin was too full of fat, to permit its contracting in to wrinkles; but from her want of teeth, weather-beaten appearance in general, and from a kind of notion that ran in my head, that nothing could have commenced at the size of infancy, and reached her present bulk in less than thirtyfive or forty years; and, in short, I was not all pleased with her.[32]

Interestingly enough, however, in the last paragraph of the letter Lincoln discussed his suffering and mortification at being turned down by Mary: "She whom I had taught myself to believe no body else would have, had actually rejected me with all my fancied greatness; and to cap the whole, I then, for the first time, began to suspect that I was really a little in love with her."[33]

In 1839 Lincoln first met and was captivated by the sprightly, well-educated, and charming Mary Todd. James C. Conkling, a young lawyer from the East and a graduate of Princeton, described Mary as "the very creature of excitement."[34] Lincoln courted her vigorously and successfully throughout 1839 and 1840. Each of her three extant letters from these two years refers to Lincoln, and apparently by 1840 there was an agreement to be married. Writing to a friend in mid-December, 1840, Mary referred several times to Lincoln and dwelled at some length on marriage: "Harriet Campbell appears to be enjoying all the sweets of married life, Mrs. Abell, came down two or three weeks since, have seen but very little of her, her silver tones, the other evening were not quite so captain like as was their wont in former times, why is it that married folks always become so serious? Miss Lamb, report says is to be married, next week, Mr Beauman I caught a glimpse of a few days, since, looked *becomingly* happy at the prospect of the change, that is about to await him, I am pleased she is about perpetrating the *crime of matrimony*, like some of our friends in *this place*." [35]

In 1840 Lincoln was thirty-one. He now had some useful experience as a lawyer behind him and was making a respectable income. He had made a mark in the legislature as a Whig and was generally esteemed by friends and colleagues throughout Springfield. He was something of a social upstart in Mary's snobbish circle—the coterie which centered in the Ninian and Elizabeth Edwards's home—and his first impression of Springfield in 1837 was of the "flourishing about in carriages here." [36] Yet he was as prepared professionally and economically for marriage as he would ever be, and his fiancée was probably the most desirable unmarried woman in Springfield. Furthermore, he had been courting Mary Todd with an apparent desire to marry her as soon as possible. Yet in a surprising move that perplexed all his friends—and has baffled historians—Lincoln broke off the engagement on January 1, 1841.

Herndon's fanciful account of the events surrounding the broken engagement [37] has been quite effectively proven false by the masterful detective work of Ruth Painter Randall. [38] Randall notes that both Mary's guardian, Ninian Edwards, and her father opposed her marriage to young Lincoln. [39] Yet he loved Mary and was engaged to her. Caught on the horns of this dilemma, Randall hypothesizes that Lincoln in the end respected the feelings of the Todd family: "How could he marry the girl when her family thought he would make her unhappy? He had so few things upon which to pride himself, but among these things was his integrity. Yet no course of action was open to a man with his torturing conscience that left that integrity unviolated." [40]

Randall's well-researched explanation is plausible and has generally become the standard account of the troubled courtship between Lincoln and Mary. As a documented chronology of events, Randall's account is not likely to be surpassed. But her explanation of Lincoln's motivation seems naïve and romantic. She speaks of Lincoln and Mary's "appealing love story" that Herndon obscured with "belittling distortions and fabrications." In Randall's view the nation can be proud of this "American romance" in which an aristocratic girl and her "lover of log-cabin origin" triumphed over family opposition. [41] It is a story in Randall's telling that evokes shades of Romeo and Juliet, American style. It posits an external force to explain Lincoln's motivation for breaking the engagement. The snobbish Todds intimidated the fragile young man, who nevertheless over time transcended his humble origins to win the hand of Mary.

Lincoln was uneasy in social situations during these years. In 1837 he felt out of place in Springfield. Throughout his life he often joked about his homeliness and excessive height. It would seem also that he felt somewhat embarrassed by his humble origins, though he later became aware of the political value of having been raised in a log cabin. Nevertheless, it would not appear that Lincoln was easily intimidated by anyone, even the snobbish Todds.[42] His natural assumption of superiority and vigorous ambition were always a source of great strength. John Hay, Lincoln's secretary during the war, wrote later that it was "absurd to call him a modest man. No great man is ever modest. It was his intellectual arrogance and unconscious assumption of superiority that men like Chase and Sumner could never forgive."[43] Lincoln was aggressively ambitious. For Herndon, the perceptive but irascible law partner, Lincoln's ambition was "a little engine that knew no rest."[44] "The sober truth is that Lincoln was inordinately ambitious."[45] The first visible expression of Lincoln's ambition, Herndon further insisted, occurred "in the year 1840 exactly."[46] But Elizabeth Edwards, Mary's sister and wife of Ninian Wirt Edwards, provided (1887) a different but also interesting explanation of the broken engagement. An important member of the family opposing the marriage, Mrs. Edwards said Lincoln "doubted his ability and capacity to please and support a wife."[47]

Elizabeth Edwards dimly perceived the excruciating ambivalence that motivated Lincoln. For as with Mary Owens, so too with Mary Todd, Lincoln broke off a fully developed romance just at the point of marriage and sexual union. In both relationships Lincoln feared intimacy—of which sexual encounter is the core experience—with a woman. His natural exuberance and virility led him into both encounters, but in each he displayed profound ambivalence which led to an agonizing retreat before consummation. To explain this curious behavior, some have even argued that Lincoln's self-doubts in sexual matters derived from a case of syphilis he supposedly contracted in 1835–36. This theory originated with the redoubtable Herndon, who claims Lincoln wrote to a Dr. Drake in Cincinnati about his disease shortly after coming to Springfield.[48] But Milton Shutes, a doctor writing in 1957, after carefully sifting all the evidence for syphilis, concluded it is virtually certain that Lincoln never contracted the disease.[49] What Shutes guessed—assuming the validity of Herndon's story—is that Lincoln developed syphilophobia. In other words, the Drake letter, which has never been found—and may never have existed—underlined Lincoln's sexual conflicts, his fears of contaminating injury to his penis. The letter, if found, would not prove prolific sexual vigor, but only sexual confusion and ignorance on the part of Lincoln. Furthermore, Lincoln was apparently a virgin when he married.[50] Syphilophobia in 1837 or 1838 was therefore a fear that had to originate in fantasy.

Intimacy involves a merging of selves—both physical and emotional—in a union that can permit each partner to rise above his or her existential loneliness. In Erik Erikson's formulation, intimacy is "the capacity to commit [oneself] to concrete affiliations and partnerships and to develop the ethical strength to abide by such commitments, even though they may call for significant sacrifices and compromises."[51] The avoidance of situations which have the potential of close affiliation and sexual union "may lead to a deep sense of isolation and consequent self-absorption."[52] For Lincoln it was precisely this loss of self that most threatened him. He could not go beyond himself because he had not fully consolidated the bases of his sexual or work identity. He lacked an inner coherence or identity that would permit him to transcend himself and reach out to another. Loss of self for such young men offers only the potential of psychic disintegration and frightening regression.

The theoretical connection between a lack of identity and a fear of intimacy is therefore far more than an accidental occurrence. Lincoln, in the 1830s, sought a unity among the several roles he was juggling: store owner, surveyor, rail-splitter, lawyer, politician. By 1841 the lawyer-politician in him seemed dominant; but it was also a recent and tentative consolidation that was neither immutable nor at the time the basis of anything more apparent than moderate professional success. He also sought a heterosexual union that somehow kept eluding him. His ego identity—his accrued confidence in an inner sameness and continuity—was fragile at best. For many less sensitive, it is all too easy to choose an identity from the available roles defined and outlined by parents, teachers, and social mores and expectations. But with Lincoln this was impossible and suggests, perhaps, an insight into a crucial aspect of greatness: the proud and obstinate refusal willingly to wear the mask painted by others. In

any event, intimacy and love are bound to be approched ambivalently for such a confused young man as Lincoln. Thus fear of intimacy
and of the binding nature of sexual love contributed to Lincoln's
identity confusion.

But Lincoln's struggle with and conflicts over intimacy cannot
fully be grasped by examining his courtship of Mary Todd alone. Of
even greater significance, perhaps, is Lincoln's relationship with
Joshua Fry Speed, whose patient friendship during these crucial
years first aggravated Lincoln's conflicts, then served as the vehicle
for their resolution. Joshua Speed was an engaging young merchant
from Kentucky who moved to Springfield in 1835. Lincoln's relationship with Speed began on his arrival in Springfield in 1837. Lincoln had only recently been admitted to the bar when he arrived, and
he had neither relatives nor friends on hand to see him through or
help him pay his debts. He was probably already acquainted with
Joshua Speed and certainly familiar with Speed's store.[53] He went
directly there and asked how much it would cost to buy the material
for a bed. Speed made the calculation and told Lincoln it would cost
a total of seventeen dollars. As Speed later reported to Herndon,
Lincoln asked for the money on credit until Christmas but in such a
sad tone as to elicit sympathy from Speed. "The tone of his voice was
so melancholy," Speed wrote, "that I felt for him. I looked up at him,
and I thought then as I think now, that I never saw so gloomy, and
melancholy a face. I said to him; 'The contraction of so small a debt,
seems to affect you so deeply, I think I can suggest a plan by which
you will be able to attain your end, without incurring any debt. I
have a very large room, and a very large double bed in it; which you
are perfectly welcome to share with me if you choose.' 'Where is
your room?' asked he. 'Upstairs' said I, pointing to the stairs leading
from the store to my room. Without saying a word, he took his sad-
dle-bags on his arm, went up stairs, set them down on the floor, came
down again, and with a face beaming with pleasure and smiles exclaimed 'Well Speed I'm moved.'"[54]

In 1838 Speed and Lincoln were joined in their room above the
store by William Herndon, who later reported: "Lincoln, Speed, and
I slept together for two or three years, i.e., slept in the same home, I
being Speed's clerk; and Lincoln sleeping with Speed."[55] For a time
Charles R. Hurst joined the dormitory, sleeping in a separate bed.[56]
Life in the store centered on open and congenial discussion and was

pervaded by a rough maleness that sharply distinguished it from the sophisticated and slightly effete atmosphere of the coterie, the salon that met in the Edwards's home.[57] According to Speed, discussion revolved around Lincoln: "Mr. Lincoln was a social man, though he did not seek company; it sought him. After he made his home with me, on every winter's night at my store, by a big wood fire, no matter how inclement the weather, eight or ten choice spirits assembled, without distinction of party. It was a sort of social club without organization. They came there because they were sure to find Lincoln."[58]

Joshua Speed was the only intimate friend Lincoln ever had. Ward Hill Lamon, in his 1872 biography, was the first to make this point.[59] The only quarrel with this assertion later came from a seemingly jealous Herndon, who also wanted to be considered an intimate friend of Lincoln.[60] In fact the difference was complete. Lincoln liked Herndon but treated him condescendingly: he always called him "Billy" while Herndon called him "Mr. Lincoln." To Speed, Lincoln wrote: "You know my desire to befriend you is everlasting— that I will never cease, while I know how to do any thing."[61] Even Herndon had to admit Lincoln and Speed were unusually close.[62] Speed was an attractive young man, affable, kind and easygoing. Ruth Randall mentions his Byronic eyes and characterizes him as a rake,[63] though the sources do not bear this out.[64] On the contrary, Speed seems to have been as innocent of sex as Lincoln, and when he began seriously courting Fanny Henning, whom he later married, Speed reported: "strange to say something of the same feeling which I regarded as so foolish in him took possession of me and kept me very unhappy from the time of my engagement until I was married."[65]

It would appear therefore that Lincoln and Speed's close relationship centered on their similar and reinforcing conflicts. Their sleeping in the same bed for three and one-half years may have intensified their closeness and aggravated their conflicts. Such close male contact during the years of Lincoln's greatest heterosexual tension seems to have heightened the difficulty he found in securing intimacy with a woman. The period during which Lincoln slept with Speed begins and ends with unconsummated female relationships, first with Mary Owens and then with Mary Todd. Speed seemed to provide an alternative relationship that neither threatened nor provoked Lincoln. Each of the two men found solace in discussing their forebodings about sexuality. Their intimate maleness substituted for the tantalizing but frightening closeness of women.

Such close male relationships were characteristic of early nineteenth-century America and were quite common in an urban frontier town such as Springfield, where there was a distinct shortage of eligible women.[66] In that pre-Freudian age, society legitimated such close male friendships, and it was not at all strange for men to sleep together in the same bed. This kind of sleeping arrangement grew out of economic necessity, and neither Speed nor Herndon found it strange. Inns at that time, with few rooms, simply separated the men from the women. Everyone crowded into all available space for warmth as much as anything else.[67] On the judicial circuit that Lincoln and other lawyers rode for some six months of every year, many charming anecdotes tell of lawyers piling into crowded beds.[68] Furthermore, spacious homes with individual chambers were extremely rare. The typical log cabin had only one room and one large bed; only when the room began to burst with children was the loft finished.

To be sure, social custom and individual biography are not always congruent. It would be clinically naïve and biographically unsophisticated to assume that because it was common for men to sleep together in the same bed it was necessarily of no significance for Lincoln that at the point of his greatest sexual tension and conflict he shared a bed with Joshua Speed. This brings us back to January 1, 1841, and the broken engagement with Mary Todd. For the event that exactly coincides with the break with Mary was the separation of Lincoln and Speed. On January 1, 1841, Speed sold his store.[69] Although he did not leave town until May, 1841, the sale of the store forced Speed and Lincoln to separate and leave their common bed.[70] It is of course conjecture, but this separation apparently threw Lincoln into a panic that severely confused his fragile sexual identity. As Erikson has noted, there is a "bisexual confusion inherent in all identity conflict."[71] In this state Lincoln's fear of intimacy with a woman was revived and to the point that he inevitably broke his engagement with Mary.

One point is worth stressing and that is the unconscious level at which Lincoln's conflicts and fears operated. He was not aware of being a conflicted young man who had delayed his psychosocial moratorium while struggling to define the dimensions of his iden-

15

tity. During the key period in this struggle as he reached thirty—which seems to be an important age for great men—he found himself sleeping for nearly four years in the same bed with another equally conflicted young man. The bonds between the two became extremely strong as they talked about politics, life, and women. On an unconscious level they came to depend on each other for recognition, affection, and support as each ventured tentatively into heterosexual relationships.

Abandoned by Speed and abandoning Mary, Lincoln fell into a severe depression, one that may even have reached suicidal proportions if we are to believe Herndon: "Did you know that Mr. Lincoln was 'as crazy as a loon' in this city in 1841; that he did not sit, did not attend to the Legislature, but in part, if any (special session of 1841); that he was then deranged? Did you know that he was forcibly arrested by his special friends here at that time; that they had to remove all razors, knives, pistols, etc. from his room and presence, that he might not commit suicide?" [72] On January 20 Lincoln wrote his friend John T. Stuart that "I have, within the last few days, been making a most discreditable exhibition of myself in the way of hypochrondriaism." Three days later, also to Stuart, Lincoln noted: "I am now the most miserable man living. If what I feel were equally distributed to the whole human family, there would not be one cheerful face on the earth." Speed confirms the deep gloom that overcame Lincoln that winter. [73] Lincoln himself came to refer to January 1, 1841, as the "fatal first," the memory of which was painful for him to recall. [74] Paul Simon, in his study of Lincoln's legislative career, has documented Lincoln's absences from the legislature that month and the fact that he was confined to his bed for the week following January 13. After that he gradually resumed his legislative duties. [75] Lincoln was of course subject to depression throughout his life, but it seems that January, 1841, was his most severe bout.

The friendship between Speed and Lincoln remained vitally important in Lincoln's emotional life during the twenty-two months after January, 1841. Speed returned to his home in Kentucky near Louisville in May, 1841. From August until mid-September Lincoln visited him there and appeared to have an enjoyable, relaxing time. [76] Lincoln returned to Springfield with Speed who remained until the end of 1842. In the thank-you letter to Speed's half sister, Mary, Lincoln mentioned Fanny Henning, whom Speed would shortly marry:

"When we left, Miss Fanny Henning was owing you a visit, as I understood. Has she paid it yet? If she has, are you not convinced that she is one of the sweetest girls in the world? There is but one thing about her, so far as I could perceive, that I would have otherwise than as it is. That is something of a tendency to melancholly. This, let it be observed, is a misfortune not a fault." [77]

In late December Speed returned to Kentucky full of self-doubt but intent on marrying Fanny.[78] Lincoln almost welcomed the appearance of his friend's dilemma and began frequently proferring advice with feeling. On January 3, 1842, Lincoln wrote Speed: "I know what the painful point with you is, at all times when you are unhappy. It is an apprehension that you do not love her as you should." [79] The following month Lincoln assured Speed: "You know my desire to befriend you is everlasting—that I will never cease, while I know how to do any thing." [80] He went on to "explain" Speed's problem: "I am now fully convinced, that you love her as ardently as you are capable of loving. Your ever being happy in her presence, and your intense anxiety about her health, if there were nothing else, would place this beyond all dispute in my mind. I incline to think it probable, that your nerves will fail you occasionally for a while; but once you get them fairly graded now, that trouble is over forever."

Lincoln thus projected his own attitudes and conflicted feelings onto Speed, through whom he vicariously reexperienced the drama he had twice played out in the previous decade. In the January 3 letter Lincoln encouraged Speed to ease his "nervous temperament" and simply let himself love Fanny: "Say candidly, were not those heavenly *black eyes*, the whole basis of all your early *reasoning* on the subject?" [81] One month later Lincoln developed the same point in the context of Speed's deep fears for Fanny's health. Lincoln imposed an interesting interpretation on Speed's anxiety, which was that it should at least assure Speed of the "truth of your affection for her." He even suggested seriously that "the Almighty has sent your present affliction expressly for that object." [82] Lincoln concluded, "Why Speed, if you did not love her, although you might not wish her death, you would most calmly by resigned to it." [83] This conclusion juxtaposing loving and killing suggests a morbid fascination with the destructive potentiality of love, sex, and marriage.

Speed's actual marriage caused Lincoln great anxiety. Lincoln wrote on February 25, 1842: "I received yours of the 12th. written the day you went down to William's place, some days since; but delayed answering it, till I should receive the promised one, of the 16th. which came last night. I opened the latter, with intense anxiety and trepidation—so much that although it turned out better than I expected, I have hardly yet, at the distance of ten hours, become calm." With clear relief Lincoln continued: "I tell you, Speed, our *forebodings*, for which you and I are rather peculiar, are all the worst sort of nonsense."[84]

Throughout Speed's courtship Lincoln had projected his own experience onto his friend in a way that permitted a vicarious reliving of his own conflicts. When Speed at last actually consummated his relationship with Fanny—and the sky did not fall in—Lincoln seemed freed as he had never been before. Within months Lincoln began secretly meeting Mary Todd again. This time, however, he brought the romance to its logical conclusion and on November 4, 1842, Lincoln married Mary Todd. But not without one last expression of the old conflicts. On October 5, 1842—a month before his marriage—Lincoln wrote Speed: "But I want to ask a closer question —'Are you now, in *feeling* as well as *judgement*, glad you are married as you are?' From any body but me, this would be an impudent question not to be tolerated, but I know you will pardon it in me. Please answer it quickly as I feel impatient to know."[85] Lincoln apparently was satisfied with Speed's answer.

In his young adulthood Lincoln sought with some difficulty to define the work and sexual dimensions of his identity. The process of definition took approximately eleven years and spanned the period between leaving his father's house and establishing his own home in earnest. Psychological characteristics are never irrevocably shaped at any stage in the life cycle. Genius in particular is elusive and a massive figure like Lincoln can never be reduced to any set of conflicts. Nor is that my intention. There are constraints, however, on emotional development that force certain problems to the surface and demand their resolution at defined stages. Identity is such a problem for adolescence and youth. For young Lincoln, the conflicts that emerged and their resolutions in these years shaped the historical figure we know. During the years of his youth Lincoln sorted out for himself, alone, the things that gave meaning and integrity to complex and at times confused strivings. These same conflicts that were so important to the young Lincoln subsequently remained significant, though less vital or actual, for the older man. Other problems intruded—raising a family, running for office, saving the nation—which Lincoln approached within the context of an identity formed during the years of his youth. In the process of finding himself, young Lincoln thus fused past and present as he prepared for what became a quite remarkable future.

TWO

Victorian Women and Domestic Life
Mary Todd Lincoln,
Elizabeth Cady Stanton, and
Harriet Beecher Stowe

KATHRYN KISH SKLAR

This essay explores themes in the private side of American life in the mid-nineteenth century—life as it was lived in houses similar to the one inhabited by Abraham and Mary Lincoln at the corner of Eighth and Jackson Streets in Springfield. In particular it explores nineteenth-century family life from the female perspective, and studies the strategies women adopted in response to change in the domestic arena.

Historians have increasingly come to see the middle decades of the nineteenth century between 1830 and 1880 as sharing a common set of social and cultural assumptions called Victorianism. In a recent essay entitled "American Victorianism as a Culture," Daniel Howe has noted that not every American was a Victorian. "American Indians, recent arrivals from the peasant societies of Europe and Asia, and the Spanish-speaking inhabitants of lands taken from Mexico," had other cultural identities, as, to a significant degree, did Afro-Americans. The reign of American Victorianism extended primarily to white, English-speaking, Protestant members of the middle class—that entrepreneurially oriented, property-owning, and capital-investing group that emerged in the late eighteenth and early nineteenth centuries a little in advance of its modern companion, the industrial proletariat.[1]

Howe and other historians are interested in the Victorian period because it, more than any other, contains the social, economic, and cultural transformations that are referred to collectively as "modernization." Victorian culture, Howe concludes, may be thought of as the culture that characterized English-speaking Americans during the climactic era of modernization when changes that had been taking shape more slowly before 1830 entered a period of accelerated development.

Profound changes in public life between 1830 and 1880 include the transportation and communication revolutions, the technologic culmination of the Industrial Revolution, and the abolition of slavery. Profound changes in family life include the widespread adoption of family limitation; the transfer of many domestic industries, such as spinning and weaving, from home to factory production; and the separation of public life and private life into two distinct spheres. Combined, these changes in family life constituted change in human history on the scale of the Neolithic Revolution.[2]

By the mid-nineteenth century when machine technology was recasting human work in unprecedented forms, human reproduction was already established on a new basis. This essay focuses on the first of these changes in Victorian families—the widespread adoption of family limitation. This essay seeks to illustrate how family limitation was integrated into the lives of three women who exemplify Victorian family planning and its various motivations: Harriet Beecher Stowe, Elizabeth Cady Stanton, and Mary Todd Lincoln. Each developed her own strategy toward, or response to, the conditions of mid-nineteenth-century family life, and each typified a strategy commonly found among her contemporaries. Harriet Beecher Stowe's strategy could be called that of "female domestic control," Elizabeth Cady Stanton's strategy that of "feminist domestic reform," and Mary Todd Lincoln's strategy that of "total commitment to husband and children." These three strategies represent the options most often pursued by Victorian women, and the contexts within which much of Victorian domestic life reverberated.

Since Harriet Beecher Stowe left behind graphic historical evidence of her private life through an exchange of letters with her husband, she makes a good beginning point for us. These letters have been quoted extensively in Edmund Wilson's *Patriotic Gore*.[3] The exchange began in the summer of 1844 when Harriet had been married for eight years, was thirty-three years old, and had borne five children, two of whom were twins. That summer, as in subsequent ones, Calvin Stowe left his Cincinnati home to raise funds in New England for Lane Theological Seminary where he taught biblical history and where his salary depended upon his summertime fund-raising efforts. Harriet and Calvin agreed to state their grievances openly to one another in their summer letters, a common practice in evangelical correspondence which usually included a good dose of mutual criticism.

Harriet's grievances began with the drudgery of nineteenth-century housework: "I am sick of the smell of sour milk and sour meat, and sour everything, and then the clothes *will* not dry, and no wet thing does, and everything smells mouldy; and altogether I feel as if I never [want] to eat again."[4] Calvin's grievances began with Harriet's aversion to the drudgery of nineteenth-century housework: "By the way there is one other thing I will mention because it has often vexed and irritated me intolerably. I must clean the stable, wash the carriage, grease the wheels, black my boots, etc. etc. but you scorn to sweep the carriage, you must always call your servant to do it and not stoop yourself to so menial an act. This makes me mad, for you are not too good to do in your line what I am everyday obliged to do in mine."[5]

Harriet's grievances included being solely responsible for running her household. Except for her, she said: "You know that . . . my unfortunate household has no mainspring, for nobody feels any kind of responsibility to do a thing in time, place, or manner, except as I oversee it."[6] On this score Calvin agreed: "You must manage all household matters in your own way—just as you would if I were dead, and you had never anything more to expect from me. Indeed, to all practical purposes I am dead for the present and know not when I shall live again."[7]

Harriet's grievances turned to the topic of her health: "As to my health, it gives me very little solicitude, although it is bad enough and daily growing worse. I feel no life, no energy, no appetite, or rather a growing distaste for food; in fact, I am becoming quite ethereal . . . I suffer with sensible distress in the brain, as I have done more or less since my sickness last winter, a distress which some days takes from me all power of planning or executing anything."[8] While not challenging his wife's claims to the symptoms and prerogatives of an invalid, and while leaving his own symptoms unnamed, Calvin obscurely asserted that his own suffering had been greater than Harriet's: "I suffer amazingly every day. I hardly know what to make of it, unless it be the Lord's penance of our sin. You have suffered a great deal, but I doubt whether you have ever suffered as I have this summer."[9]

In addition to these everyday grievances, husband and wife discussed a larger problem in the summer of 1844—their sexual relationship. Calvin broached the topic by relating several recent instances of clerical disarray in the sexual arena, including the story of a fellow minister who "While half boozled [had] caught young ladies who were so unfortunate to meet him alone, and pawed them over in the most disgusting manner, and actually attempted to do them physical violence. This has been going on for years until it would be borne no longer, and now it all comes out against him, to the dishonor of religion, his own unspeakable shame and anguish, and the distress unutterable of his wife and children."[10] In connection with this "melancholy licentiousness" Calvin said he had "thought much of our domestic happiness," and in a paragraph packed with homesickness he drew both a parallel and a contrast between himself and his fallen colleagues, beginning:

Though I have, as you well know, a most enthusiastic admiration of fresh, youthful female beauty; yet it never comes anywhere near the kind of feeling I have for you. With you, every desire I have, mental and physical, is completely satisfied and filled up, and leaves me nothing more to ask for. My enjoyment with you is not weakened by time nor blunted with age, and every reunion after separation is just as much of a honeymoon as was the first month after the wedding. Is not your own experience and observation a proof of what I say? . . . No man can love and respect his wife more than I do mine. Yet we are not happy as we might be.

Let us look at the place the summer of 1844 occupied in the sequence of Harriet Beecher Stowe's childbearing to see if we can understand better why she and Calvin were "not as happy" as they might have been, in spite of Calvin's testimony to their sexual compatibility. For that summer may not have been a time when Harriet wanted to relive her honeymoon, but a time when she was looking forward to what she considered a well-earned relief from giving birth. Such relief had not been possible for her mother, since most women who were married before 1800 bore children, in sickness and in health, regularly every two years from the time they married to the end of their childbearing years, or until their death, whichever came first. But limitation of childbearing was an option for Harriet—one she had considered long before the summer of 1844.

Harriet Beecher married Calvin Stowe in 1836 at the age of twenty-six after she had nearly ten years' experience supporting herself as a teacher. One hopes that his bride shared Calvin's high esteem for their honeymoon, since nine months after their marriage—almost to the day—Harriet gave birth to twins. Then, a few months later she was pregnant again. At this point she was visited by her reform-minded older sister, Catharine Beecher, who later described Harriet's plight in a letter to another married sister: "Harriet has one baby put out for the winter, the other at home, and number three will be here the middle of January. Poor thing, she bears up wonderfully well and I hope will live through this first tug of matrimonial warfare, and then she says she shall not have any more *children*, *she knows for certain* for one while. Though how she found this out I cannot say, but she seems quite confident about it." [11]

The outcome of matrimonial warfare in the Stowe family during the next five years was the addition of two more babies, the second born in the summer of 1843. This second baby was sickly and languished in Harriet's arms all fall and winter while she herself suffered through a prolonged illness related, apparently, to the birth. A year later, in the summer of 1844, Harriet replied to Calvin's amorous letter and to his descriptions of clerical licentiousness with one of the finest passages of Victorian domestic prose I know. Assuming that sexual infidelity was unjustified on any grounds, and taking up the implicit threat contained in Calvin's admission of his "most enthusiastic admiration of fresh, youthful female beauty," Harriet dramatized her horror at the possibility of Calvin's infidelity, but she did not respond in kind to his suggestions that marital love was better than burning.

As I am gifted with a most horrible vivid imagination, in a moment I imagined—nay saw as in a vision all the distress and despair that would follow a fall on your part. I felt weak and sick—I took a book and lay down on the bed, but it pursued me like a nightmare—and something seemed to ask Is your husband any better seeming than so and so! I looked in the glass and my face which since spring has been something of the palest was so haggard that it frightened me. The illusion lasted a whole forenoon and then evaporated like a poisonous mist—but God knows how I pity those heart wrung women—wives worse than widows, who are called to lament that the grave has not covered their husband—the father of their children! Good and merciful God—why are such agonies reserved for the children of men![12]

Dwelling on the vividness, intensity, and even sublimity of her horror for a moment, Harriet continued: "I can conceive now of misery which in one night would change the hair to grey and shrivel the whole frame to premature decrepitude! misery to which all other agony is as a mocking sound!" Then, with a brief reference to Calvin's sex, Harriet launched into a discussion of their marital love from her point of view.

What terrible temptations lie in the way of your sex—till now I never realised it—for tho I did love you with an almost *insane* love before I married you I never knew yet or felt the pulsation which showed me I could be tempted in that way—there never was a moment when I felt anything by which you could have drawn me astray—for I loved you as I now love God—and I can conceive of no higher love; and as I have no passion, I have no jealousy. The most beautiful woman in the world could not make me jealous so long as she only *dazzled the senses*.

Calvin might declare his love for Harriet as "mental and physical," but Harriet made it clear to him that it was not for his body that she loved him. She would admit to insanity before she would admit to sexual desire. In the spring of 1845 Harriet left Calvin at home to manage the household as best he could while she spent ten months at a Brattleboro, Vermont, water cure. Almost immediately upon her return home, Calvin departed for fifteen months of water cure himself.

From Brattleboro Harriet described to Calvin her analysis of their situation: "We have now come to a sort of crisis. If you and I do as we should for *five years* to come the character of our three oldest children will be established. This is why I am willing to spend so much time and make such efforts to have health. Oh, that God would give me these five years in full possession of mind and body, that I may train my children as they should be trained." Harriet may have related "full possession of mind and body" to the adoption of "system and order" in family life, for she immediately continued: "I am fully aware of the importance of system and order in a family. I know that nothing can be done without it; it is the keystone, the *sine qua non*, and in regard to my children I place it next to piety."[13]

For six years from 1843 to 1849, Harriet Beecher Stowe avoided pregnancy. After bearing children in a pattern that resembled her mother's up to the age of thirty-two, she enjoyed a long span of childlessness that was unknown to most women of her mother's generation, but quite common among Harriet's contemporaries. Her mother, Roxana Beecher, gave birth to nine children in seventeen years of marriage before she died at the age of thirty-seven. Harriet bore five children in the first seven years of marriage, none in the second six years of marriage, and two more at the end of her child-bearing years, in 1849 and 1850, when she was thirty-eight and thirty-nine. She therefore omitted two to three children that her mother would not have omitted, and in this time before artificial contraceptive techniques, she must have relied largely on sexual abstinence.

How typical was the childbearing pattern of this distinguished nineteenth-century author who produced her most famous book the same year she birthed her last baby?

The timing of Elizabeth Cady Stanton's children was very similar to that of Harriet Beecher Stowe's. She had three in the first five years of marriage, then, like Harriet, went six years without bearing children. It was toward the end of this interval between 1845 and 1851 that she began her campaign for woman's rights. Then, during the eight years from 1851 to 1859, she gave birth to four more babies, the last when she was forty-four years old.[14]

Harriet Beecher Stowe, Elizabeth Cady Stanton, and, as we will see, Mary Todd Lincoln were all participating in Victorian family planning—a phenomenon that had begun in New England before they were born, and that had, by the time they were married between 1835 and 1845, become (for reasons that still elude historical explanation) a much-accelerated national trend, most emphatically felt in middle-class families, but affecting all economic groups, both urban and rural. Victorian families were deeply involved in what is called the "demographic transition"—a shift from the high birth and high death rates characteristic of traditional populations, to the low birth and low death rates characteristic of our own twentieth-century population. More people lived longer, so the population as a whole grew rapidly, but fewer babies were born to individual women. Whereas the average number of children born to women who survived to age forty was seven to eight in 1800, in 1900 it was less than half that number and still falling rapidly.[15]

Up until about ten years ago historians attributed this reduction in family size to industrialization and urbanization. Thanks to the statistical techniques developed by French demographer Louis Henry in the 1950s, and the application of these techniques to American data in the last ten years, we have learned that the origins of modern family limitation predate significant industrialization and urbanization—in France by almost a century; in the United States by at least a generation. Many questions remain to be answered about the connections between economic and demographic change in the first half of the nineteenth century. But since we now know that family limitation was widespread throughout Victorian society before 1850, when industrialization and urbanization had barely begun, these latter forces no longer explain the emergence of marital fertility control. In a recent article entitled "Family History and Demographic Transition," Robert Wells argues that family limitation was the result of "modern attitudes"—the belief that "the world is knowable and controllable" and that it serves one's own interests to plan one's life.[16]

Harriet Beecher Stowe's matrimonial warfare would seem to fall in this category of thinking, as did her strategy of asserting female control in the sexual arena. In addition, invalidism and Victorian sexuality were not the only means Harriet used to control her circumstances rather than be controlled by them. In a letter to a close friend shortly after Catharine's visit in 1838, she described the full scope of her domestic self-assertion: "I have about three hours per day in writing, and if you see my name coming out everywhere you may be sure of one thing, that I *do* it *for the pay*. I have determined not to be a mere domestic slave without even the leisure to excel in my duties. I mean to have money enough to have my house kept in the best manner and yet to have time for reflection and that preparation for the education of my children which every mother needs. I have every prospect of succeeding in this plan."[17]

Harriet Beecher Stowe was a unique and gifted woman whose novel dramatizing the effects of slavery on family life made her more famous than representative among her contemporaries, but the general circumstances of her domestic life were widely shared. Another young mother living five hundred miles away in western New York, Elizabeth Cady Stanton, approached her domestic responsibilities with the same modern effort to plan and control the outcome. As Stanton described her response to motherhood in 1842 in her autobiography: "Having gone through the ordeal of bearing a child, I was determined if possible to keep him, so I read everything I could find on the subject."[18] One of the manuals Stanton might have come across in her search for pediatric guidance was Catharine Beecher's *Treatise on Domestic Economy*, first published in 1841, reprinted every year until 1856, and distributed nationally by Harper and Brothers. For Beecher's *Treatise*, the most important fact in a woman's life was not whether she was pious or loving, but whether she controlled her own life, for "there is nothing, which so distinctly marks the difference between weak and strong minds, as the fact, whether they control circumstances, or circumstances control them."[19]

Not passive submission to their biological identity nor fetching dependence on their husbands, but active control of their immediate life circumstances was the model Harriet's sister held out to her readers. Adopting a typical Victorian perspective, Beecher viewed motherhood as a qualitative rather than a quantitative activity, useful to society for the kind of child rather than the numbers of children it produced. In a chapter entitled "The Peculiar Responsibilities of American Women," she wrote: "The success of democratic institutions, as is conceded by all, depends upon the intellectual and moral character of the mass of the people. If they are intelligent and virtuous, democracy is a blessing; but if they are ignorant and wicked, it is only a curse. It is equally conceded, that the formation of the moral and intellectual character of the young is committed mainly to the female hand."[20] Beecher's view of the relationship between childhood and society was an essentially modern one. Rather than viewing society as a traditional set of established controls, and early childhood as a time when the will must be broken to conform to those controls, she saw society as an uncontrolled growth, except as it was regulated by the internalized values of "character" developed during early childhood. Seeing it possible to exert in early childhood an influence of lifelong personal and social significance, Victorians were far more sensitive than their ancestors had been to the importance of the right kind of mothering.

Qualitative motherhood and the elevated status it brought Victorian women could be the basis for initiating improvements in other aspects of female life. For Beecher it justified an appeal for the advance of female education. As her *Treatise* stated: "Are not the most responsible of all duties committed to the charge of woman? Is it not her profession to take care of mind, body, and soul? and that, too, at the most critical of all periods of existence? And is it not as much a matter of public concern, that she should be properly qualified for her duties, as that ministers, lawyers, and physicians, should be prepared for theirs? And is it not as important, to endow institutions which shall make a superior education accessible to all classes—for females, as much as for the other sex?" [21]

But for some Victorian women, qualitative motherhood and the female control and assertion we have seen Harriet Beecher Stowe exercise and Catharine Beecher advocate for women in the domestic arena, did not go far enough. Basic inequalities of status between men and women still intruded sharply into domestic life. Married women could not, without special legal efforts, own property, and their earnings belonged to their husbands. Lincoln's willingness to include females in the extension of suffrage to all tax-paying or arms-bearing citizens, as described by Professor Roy Basler's essay in this volume, would therefore have affected very few women—primarily spinsters and widows. [22] Responding to these and other limitations of nineteenth-century domesticity, Elizabeth Cady Stanton decided to do something in 1848. As she described her state of mind prior to organizing the first Woman's Rights Convention:

The general discontent I felt with woman's portion as wife, mother, housekeeper, physician, and spiritual guide, the chaotic conditions into which everything fell without her constant supervision, and the wearied, anxious look of the majority of women impressed me with a strong feeling that some active measure should be taken. My experience at the World's Anti-Slavery Convention, all I had read of the legal status of women, and the oppression I saw everywhere, swept across my soul intensified now by many personal experiences . . . I could not see what to do or where to begin—my only thought was a public meeting for protest and discussion. [23]

While the growth of female autonomy, power, and control within the home was an important component of Victorian domesticity, one of the central tenets of Victorian family life—its separation from the public sphere—prohibited women from exercising outside the domestic world the influence they held within it. Thus the family world of Victorian women was half full or half empty, depending on how one looked at it—half full in providing the potential for the assertion of control over one's life, or half empty in denying to women the legal, political, and economic rights that men enjoyed. For Harriet Beecher Stowe it was half full and she worked to fill it more completely through her writings. For Elizabeth Cady Stanton it was half empty and would only be adequately filled when women were recognized legally and politically as people, rather than the "female relatives of people." [24]

While Harriet Beecher Stowe represents one common female response to the changing conditions of domestic life in taking the initiative to control and plan her life, and Stanton represents a reform strategy in response to the same conditions, Mary Todd Lincoln represents a strategy of total commitment to husband and children.

In her we see a slightly different and even more modern pattern of childbearing than we have seen in Stowe or Stanton. Lincoln's wife, like Calvin Stowe's, bore her first baby a neat nine months after marriage.[25] Mary Todd Lincoln, however, subsequently maintained what seems to have been a more controlled and more even spacing of her children than either Stowe or Stanton and she ceased bearing children altogether at a much earlier age than Harriet or Elizabeth. After an interval of nearly three years between her first and second child, Mary was not pregnant again until four years later when her second child, Edward, died and her third, Willie, was immediately conceived. After another interval of three years between her third and fourth births, Mary Lincoln ceased bearing children altogether when she was only thirty-five years old.

With babies born in 1843, 1846, 1850, and 1853, Mary Todd Lincoln gave less of her own life cycle to the reproductive life of the species than either Harriet Beecher Stowe or Elizabeth Cady Stanton. Mary Todd's mother had given birth regularly every other year after her marriage until she died from causes related to the birth of her seventh when Mary was six years old. Mary's stepmother followed the same traditional pattern, bearing ten children in all, with shorter intervals between births and continuing childbearing well beyond her mid-thirties. But Mary's pattern of childbearing was quite different.

Whereas family limitations for Stowe and Stanton was an on-again, off-again activity, concentrated in a six-year interval in the middle of their childbearing years, Mary Lincoln's family limitation seems to have begun soon after her first child was born, and to have gained momentum in 1847, the year after her second child was born and the year when Lincoln was first elected to Congress. Over the course of the eleven years between 1847 and 1858 when Mrs. Lincoln was twenty-nine to forty years old, she conceived only two children, although her mother's pattern would have produced five children in that length of time.

The greater effectiveness and longevity of fertility control in the Lincoln family seems to suggest the cooperation of husband and wife in the effort. Mary and Abraham Lincoln may exemplify a different kind of family-limitation motivation than the female initiative we saw with Harriet and Calvin Stowe. In many Victorian families, probably including the Lincolns, we can assume that husbands as well as wives viewed their economic betterment or professional advancement as more important than the biblical imperative to "be fruitful and multiply."

We might, indeed, see the bias toward sexual abstinence that Victorian sexual ideology promoted in women as a kind of "fail-safe" protection against the victory of instinct over economic self-interest, and as positive reinforcement for what was, in any case, a necessity of everyday life. In many families husbands and wives may have been in complete agreement about their priorities and have placed the husband's advancement high among these. This certainly seems to have been the case with Mary and Abraham Lincoln.

Nineteenth-century "togetherness" was nowhere better exemplified than in the Lincoln family. All the basic components were there. In their devotion to their children, both Mary and Abraham were making up for unhappy childhoods, loving their sons in ways that compensated for their own maternal deprivation, both having lost their mothers before they were ten years old. The Lincolns indulged their children notoriously, but they had other ambitions that limited the number of children they could raise with such devotion. Until he was elected to the U.S. Congress in 1847, Lincoln's career ambitions in law and politics meant that he was away from home as frequently as he was present, and after his election the Lincoln's home life was even more disrupted. But Mary Lincoln endorsed her husband's career ambitions and gave them top priority in their mutual family life. In 1860 the Lincoln home was an important political meeting ground. As Mrs. Lincoln wrote a friend: "This summer we have had immense crowds of strangers visiting us, and have had no time to be occupied with home affairs." [26]

Perhaps even more important than the terms on which Lincoln

family life proceeded were those under which the marriage had begun. In contrast to Harriet Beecher and Elizabeth Cady, Mary Todd married against her family's wishes. Whereas Harriet and Elizabeth both married protégés of their fathers, and both bore their first child in their parents' home, Mary encountered considerable opposition to her marriage from her sister and brother-in-law, Elizabeth Todd Edwards and Ninian Wirt Edwards, who were her de facto guardians in Springfield. The Edwards did not try to hide their disapproval of a marriage they thought was beneath Mary Todd's social standing, and their attitude may have contributed to Lincoln's decision to break off the engagement in 1841. Mary bore her first child in Springfield's Globe Tavern, assisted by her husband rather than her sister, even though her sister lived within walking distance. Marrying for love against the wishes of her family, enduring poverty in early marriage after a wealthy upbringing, but never losing faith in the promise of her husband's career, Mary Lincoln's marriage was in many ways the very model of a nineteenth-century romantic love success story.

But Mary Lincoln's commitment to her husband and children generated trauma as well as joy in her life. One might go as far as to say that her psychological "untogetherness" was reciprocally related to the modern "togetherness" in her family life. With so much love invested in her children, she was spiritually broken with the death of four-year-old Edward in 1850; and although she was pregnant a month after Edward's death and replaced the child numerically immediately, qualitatively the child was irreplaceable to her. It was after Edward's death, when she was thirty-two years old, that she began to lose control of her life. As Justin Turner and Linda Turner wrote in their superb edition of Mrs. Lincoln's letters: "The humor and control that had sustained her in the past became increasingly submerged in fearfulness, self-indulgence, and in sudden outbursts of rage."[27] While Mary suffered deep emotional wounds with the loss of Edward, Abraham Lincoln emerged from the crisis with a new spiritual strength and resilience. As the Turners described Lincoln's resolution of this crisis: "The man who was by nature melancholy, solitary, and self-doubting would from then on gain in assurance and magnetism."[28]

The deepest and most intense glimpse we have into Mary Lincoln's domestic commitment and childbearing experience comes from a letter written by Circuit Judge David Davis while he and Lincoln were riding the Eighth Judicial Circuit in June 1852. Davis wrote to his wife Sarah: "Lincoln got a letter from his wife. She says . . . [her baby] has the nursing sore mouth—child 18 mos. old. I guess she ought to have quit nursing some time ago."[29]

The baby whom Mary was nursing so long as to imperil his health in June 1852 was Willie, born in late December, 1850, approximately nine months after Eddie's death that same year. Tad was born ten months after Davis wrote this letter to his wife. Mary Lincoln apparently conceived her fourth and last son the month after she weaned her third, who had in turn been conceived less than one month after the death of her second son. This concentrated bout of childbearing and nursing between 1850 and 1853 seems to have been prompted by Eddie's death, and in the case of Willie's "nursing sore mouth," seems to have been prompted by irrational as well as rational motivations.

The death of this second son, twelve-year-old William in 1862, drove Mary Lincoln across the boundary between this world and the spirit world. She began to see visions of Willie and Edward standing at the foot of her bed, and, after an incomplete recovery, she launched on a compulsive and disastrous effort to make up for her loss by buying clothes, jewels, and household furnishings she could not afford, accumulating twenty thousand dollars in personal debts Lincoln did not know about at the time of his death.[30]

Whereas Harriet Beecher Stowe and Elizabeth Cady Stanton participated in the active and extensive female subculture contained within Victorian society, Stowe through her writing and Stanton through her reform activities, Mary Lincoln's activities outside the domestic arena tended to reinforce the centrality of her husband in her life.

Socially her circle of Springfield friends and kin called "the coterie," was dominated by her sister and brother-in-law, Elizabeth and Ninian Edwards, and since it was Elizabeth and Ninian who had initially obstructed her marriage, Mary's participation in Springfield social life was accompanied by the need to prove the wisdom of her marriage and the brilliance of her husband. Ninian Edwards was the son of the territorial governor and first U.S. senator of Illinois. The exclusive aristocratic circle he and Elizabeth Todd Edwards constructed in Springfield continued the integration of politics and family life that Elizabeth and Mary Todd had known as children in Lexington, Kentucky. There the Todds were one of the most politically active and important Whig families in the region. For Mary Todd the ebb and flow of state and national politics was a central ingredient of family life. As a girl she had exchanged political banter with Henry Clay. After she went to live with Elizabeth and Ninian Edwards in Springfield and was in the thick of her courtship with Lincoln at the age of twenty-two, she wrote to a friend about the election of 1840: "This fall I became quite a *politician*, rather an unladylike profession, yet at such a *crisis*, whose heart could remain untouched while the energies of all were called in question?"[31]

After her marriage Mary Todd channeled this enthusiasm for party politics into the support of her husband's career. She had taken a great risk in marrying Lincoln—a far greater risk than either Harriet Beecher or Elizabeth Cady took in their marriages—and every contribution she made to her husband's career was a contribution to the justification of that risk. As a result she strongly identified with and took great personal satisfaction in her husband's career advancement. After Lincoln met Douglas in their historic debates in 1858, Mrs. Lincoln characteristically declared: "Mr. Douglas is a very, little, little giant by the side of my tall Kentuckian, and intellectually my husband towers above Douglas just as he does physically."[32]

For Mary Todd Lincoln the doctrine of separate spheres did not apply. Her unladylike participation in the political arena, in the name of defending or advancing her husband's interests, earned her many enemies while she occupied the White House; but, for her, family life, political life, and social life were a single unit organized around her husband. There was a great deal of truth to her description of him as "lover—husband—father & *all all to me*—truly my all."[33]

In the 1860s the intersection of historical events and life strategies placed Harriet Beecher Stowe, Elizabeth Cady Stanton, and Mary Todd Lincoln in very different circumstances. After her husband's assassination Mary Lincoln was paralyzed with grief, was ever thereafter only in fleeting contact with reality, and was unable to defend herself against William Herndon's claims that she and Lincoln had never loved one another.

Harriet Beecher Stowe, by contrast, after being very deeply shaken by the death of her eldest son at the age of nineteen in 1857, purged her despair and her fear for his afterlife in a novel set in the religious New England of her childhood, and through that novel moved from slavery to New England traditional life as the setting for her mature and best fiction. The interaction between Harriet's domestic life and her writing contained a built-in dynamic of growth, as through her writing she gained strength to endure family calamity, and through family loss she improved her writing.[34] Her 1858 novel, *The Minister's Wooing*, (written after her son's sudden death) explored the similarities between Christ's love and a mother's love and concluded that her unconverted son could not be in hell because she (and therefore the Redeemer) loved him so much. There was no such built-in dynamic of growth or satisfactory resolution of death in Mary Lincoln's life, which seriously lost momentum and coherence after the death of each child in 1850 and 1862. Three years before her husband's assassination and nine years before the final blow of the death of eighteen-year-old Tad in 1871, Mary Lincoln wrote to a friend: "My question to myself is, 'Can life be endured?'"[35] In 1875 she was committed as a "lunatic" to a sanitarium for women in Batavia, Illinois, by her only living son, Robert.

The contrast between Harriet Beecher Stowe and Mary Todd Lincoln is one between a Victorian woman who was able to build an autonomous self within the domestic arena and a woman who was not able to do so. The contrast between Stowe and Stanton is less marked, being between a Victorian wife and mother who was interested in portraying the private side of domestic life and therefore remained primarily a private person, and a Victorian wife and mother who wanted to portray and change the public policies governing domestic life and therefore grew into a public personage. Both women wrote at home, amid the play and interruptions of their children. Stanton, who after 1851 at the age of thirty-six began to spend a good deal of her life in public, bore four more chilren at the same time— two more than Harriet Stowe and four more than Mary Lincoln bore after that age.

Stanton had help in sustaining this double commitment to family and public life. Indeed, one might say that after 1851 she lived in two marriages—one to Henry B. Stanton, one to Susan B. Anthony. Anthony came to visit Stanton often after they met in 1851, and their mutually supportive relationship formed the core of the woman's rights movement for almost fifty years. As Stanton described the relationship in her autobiography:

We never met without issuing a pronunciamento on some question. In thought and sympathy we were one, and in the division of labor we exactly complemented each other. . . . We have indulged freely in criticism of each other when alone, and hotly contended whenever we have differed, but in our friendship of years there has never been the break of one hour. To the world we always seem to agree and uniformly reflect each other. Like husband and wife, each has the feeling that we must have no differences in public. Thus united at an early day we began to survey the state and nation, the future field of our labors.[36]

As Stanton described their equal division of domestic work: "We took turns on the domestic watchtowers, directing amusements, settling disputes, protecting the weak against the strong, and trying to secure equal rights to all in the home as well as the nation."

Our historical view of American women in the Victorian era has been shaped by Barbara Welter's pioneering 1966 article, "The Cult of True Womanhood, 1820–1860," which delineated the era's primary demands of female purity, piety, submissiveness, and domesticity.[37] Since then Carroll Smith-Rosenberg, Nancy F. Cott, and other scholars have explored these themes further and found that female purity or "passionlessness" had positive effects on the lives of many Victorian women; that religion and female piety could act as a basis for collective action in behalf of female interests; and that domesticity itself was not an empty set of prescriptions for idle women, but a vocation that complemented the career ambitions of nineteenth-century men.[38]

The three women discussed here have shown these modernizing trends in nineteenth-century family life. Although each responded differently to the demands of qualitative motherhood, each represented a common strategy found among her contemporaries. Stowe's strategy of female control in the domestic arena was a mainstream strategy shared by the domestic feminism of thousands, perhaps tens of thousands, of New England and New York women who joined the American Female Moral Reform Society between 1840 and 1860—an organization founded in the 1830s with the sole purpose of eliminating prostitution and the double sexual standard on which it was based. This militant grassroots movement identified in their weekly newspaper, the *Advocate of Moral Reform*, eminent men who frequented brothels. The *Advocate* boasted a circulation of 16,500 in the late 1830s, making it the most widely-read evangelical newspaper in the country.[39]

Stanton's strategy of feminist domestic reform was less widespread than Stowe's brand of domestic feminism, but it was more radical. In her recent book, *Feminism and Suffrage, the Emergence of an Independent Women's Movement in America, 1848–1869,* Ellen Carol DuBois argued that the basic premises informing Stanton and Anthony's leadership of the women's rights movement "were the necessity of revolutionary change in women's position and the conviction that other women could come to understand and demand that change."[40] The title of Stanton and Anthony's first newspaper, *Revolution,* supports this view, while at the same time it reveals their appreciation of the difficulties involved in achieving their goal of full citizenship for women and the legal equality of the sexes.

Mary Lincoln's strategy of fulfilling her own personal ambition vicariously through husband and children was another mainstream strategy—one that enjoys continued popularity in the last quarter of the twentieth century. Women married to men with political careers still find it especially difficult to pursue autonomous life goals.

Representing the most common options open to mid-nineteenth-century women, the life strategies of Stowe, Stanton, and Lincoln brought them into indirect conflict with one another at the end of the Civil War. Stowe advocated a thorough reconstruction of Southern life. Stanton lobbied for the incorporation of women in the postwar extension of civil rights through the Fourteenth and Fifteenth amendments. Mary Lincoln was by that time even more irrationally protective of and loyal to her husband since that loyalty now carried with it not only the justification of her marriage but the justification of the battlefield slaying of her Southern kin. Although their interests briefly intersected in 1865 when all three were pressuring Senator Charles Sumner to support their perspective, the trajectories of their lives soon carried them in quite different directions. It is tragic and ironic that Mary Lincoln, who committed herself most completely to modern notions of female fulfillment through family in the 1840s and 1850s, was in the late 1860s displaced in the public mind by her husband's mythical romance with Ann Rutledge. After 1865 Stowe's and Stanton's lives carried them further outside the domestic arena, and they remained public figures for another thirty years. One important aspect of their achievement was their ability to integrate their public and domestic lives in ways that supported and sustained them as mothers, wives, and individuals.

THREE

Lincoln, Blacks, and Women

ROY P. BASLER

It is difficult to write on any historical subject without awareness of how our national successes and failures, satisfactions and dissatisfactions, all seem to flourish on the roots our forefathers put down in 1776. That the Declaration of Independence is the taproot no one will deny, even when ignoring the present-day implications of the "self-evident truths" which, thanks to Thomas Jefferson's phraseology, were and are the moral justification of our national political existence. Most of us will also agree that Jefferson's concept of human equality was and is the shibboleth by which Americans test the sincerity or hypocrisy of our leaders, our institutions, and occasionally in rare moments of truth, even of ourselves. The Declaration was the "rebuke and a stumbling-block to the very harbingers of reappearing tyranny and oppression," as Abraham Lincoln described it.[1] It was also his principal maxim, both as a man and as a politician who became president, whenever he confronted the two classes of human beings whom the laws of the land did not recognize as either free or equal—blacks and women.

When President Lincoln's Proclamation freed the slaves in the Confederate states, reactions among Southerners as well as Northerners, slaves as well as the free, were, as might be expected, pessimistic or optimistic depending on the individual. In South Carolina, discussion of the future which lay before its citizens seems to have been a continuing activity even at the afternoon teas of the ladies. Mary Boykin Chesnut recorded in her *Diary* that the wife of Gen. Joseph E. Johnston said that she had been opposed to slavery, although her husband was not. Mrs. Chesnut replied that she too was opposed to slavery and that her husband, "Mr. Chesnut . . . hates all slavery, especially African slavery." Mrs. Johnston asked, "Why do you say 'African'?" Mrs. Chesnut replied, "Why, to distinguish that form from the inevitable slavery of the world. All married women, all children and girls who live in the father's houses are slaves!"[2]

On another occasion, Mary Chesnut elaborated on the status of women. "South Carolina as a rule does not think it necessary for women to have any existence outside of their pantries or nurseries. . . . The pleasures of all the world are reserved for men."[3] She returned to the subject again and again:

We whimper and whine, they say, we speak in a deprecating voice, and sigh gently at the end of every sentence. . . . Does a man ever speak to his wife and children except to find fault? Does a woman ever address any remark to her husband that does not begin with an excuse? When a man does wrong, does not his wife have to excuse herself if he finds out she knows it? If a man drinks too much, and his wife shows that she sees it, what a storm she brings about her ears! She is disrespectful, unwomanly, so unlike her mother, so different from the women of his family. Do you wonder that we are afraid to raise our voices above a mendicant's moan?[4]

This state of affairs was by no means limited to South Carolina, although perhaps more exaggerated there than elsewhere. It had been so throughout the United States from the nation's beginning. At the very time Thomas Jefferson was discussing with colleagues such as John Adams the wording of the Declaration of Independence, Abigail Adams was writing to her husband, "I long to hear that you have declared an independency. And by the way, in the new code of laws which I suppose it will be necessary for you to make, I desire you would remember the ladies and be more generous and favorable to them than your ancestors. Do not put such unlimited power into the hands of husbands. Remember, all men would be tyrants if they could. If particular care and attention is not paid to the ladies, we are determined to foment a rebellion, and will not hold ourselves bound by any laws in which we have no voice or representation."[5]

John Adams would qualify as a male chauvinist in terms used by modern feminists, for he dismissed his wife's suggestion as a big joke: "As to your extraordinary code of laws, I cannot but laugh. . . . Depend upon it, we know better than to repeal our masculine systems. Although they are in full force, you know they are little more than theory. We dare not exert our power in its full latitude. We are obliged to go fair and softly, and, in practice, you know we are the subjects. We have only the name of masters, and rather than give up this, which would completely subject us to the despotism of the petticoat, I hope General Washington and all our brave heroes would fight; I am sure every good politican would plot, as long as he would against despotism, empire, monarchy, aristocracy, oligarchy, or ochlocracy. A fine story indeed!"[6]

Abigail had the last, if futile word, in this seriocomic exchange, which would be only the more comic if we had not already heard Mary Chesnut's sad words on the subject written nearly a century later. Abigail wrote back, "I cannot say that I think you are very generous to the ladies; for, whilst you are proclaiming peace and goodwill to men, emancipating all nations, you insist upon retaining an absolute power over wives. But you must remember that arbitrary power is like most other things which are very hard, very liable to be broken."[7]

Thus, in the early nineteenth century, inequality of women came to be, along with African slavery, one-half of a dual black-white target for shafts of rhetoric aimed by would-be reformers. Many, if not all, abolitionists were also advocates of rights for women. Not only the women—Susan B. Anthony, Lucretia Mott, Elizabeth Cady Stanton, Harriet Beecher Stowe, and the Grimké sisters, Angelina and Sarah, to name only a few of the many women activists—but also the men—William Lloyd Garrison, Theodore Weld, Lewis Tappan, and perhaps the greatest of all, the mulatto ex-slave Frederick Douglass—were advocates of both equal rights for women and the abolition of slavery. Black abolitionists in their early more or less segregated conventions declared their belief in the equality of the sexes and in 1848 issued an invitation to "females hereafter to take part in our deliberations."[8] Their aim was almost unanimously dual, but their priorities and programs for action were so diverse that it would be impossible to summarize them adequately for the purposes here.

That one of these two objectives came to obscure, if not obliterate, the other in the march of political events in the 1830s was not the choice of the resolute reformers. It resulted from the conflict of economic and political interests assumed by the slavocracy on the one side and the industrial-agricultural system based on free and cheap labor on the other. The struggle between slavery and antislavery gradually banished nearly every other issue from the public mind between 1830 and 1860 when Abraham Lincoln was elected president by an antislavery electorate concentrated in the Northern half of the Union.

Lincoln's position regarding slavery was elaborated in so many speeches and writings between 1830 and 1860 that it is probably unnecessary even to summarize, but for the record let us review. In 1837 he stated his belief, "that the institution of slavery is founded on both injustice and bad policy; but that the promulgation of abolition doctrines tends rather to increase than to abate its evils. . . . that the Congress of the United States has no power, under the constitution, to interfere with the institution of slavery in the different States . . . that the Congress of the United States has the power, under the constitution, to abolish slavery in the District of Columbia; but that that power ought not to be exercised unless at the request of the people of said District."[9] To this limited statement of 1837 we should add his belief that Congress not only could prevent, but had already prevented, the extension of slavery into the territories north of the line agreed upon in the Missouri Compromise of 1820. When this was modified by Henry Clay's Compromise of 1850, Lincoln expressed no objection. But with the enactment of Stephen A. Douglas's Kansas-Nebraska Act in 1854, he became one of the leading political opponents of slavery extension, and on this issue alone was elected president in 1860.

Among the many forceful and even emotional statements of his personal belief, one made in a speech at Chicago on July 10, 1858, may be allowed here to stand for all the others as the avowal which most succinctly stated his belief: "I say in relation to the principle that all men are created equal, let it be as nearly reached as we can."[10]

At this point let us drop back again a quarter of a century and consider what Lincoln's position was on the question of equal rights for women. First of all, it must be admitted that unlike the question of the abolition of slavery, the question of "rights for women" was not looming very large in Illinois politics, nor, so far as I have learned, in the personal views of either men or women as they were locally recorded. Nevertheless, it is a notable fact that Lincoln's published statement of political views in the *Sangamo Journal*, June 13, 1836, avowed specifically: "I go for all sharing the privileges of the government, who assist in bearing its burthens. Consequently I go for admitting all whites to the right of suffrage, who pay taxes or bear arms, (by no means excluding females)." [11] In this statement Lincoln was far ahead of most of his political contemporaries, and by no means behind even the crusading feminists and abolitionists of the day. Since, so far as I can find, he had nothing further to say on the subject, we may assume that he thought he had settled the matter in his own mind once and for all. At any rate, until the question of slavery was settled, people at large in the United States could not give much attention to woman suffrage, or any other social reform. Even Dorothea Dix's strenuous campaign for reform of insane asylums was very slow to obtain results. Although she managed to get bills through several state legislatures, her bill to obtain federal money for care of the insane, finally passed by Congress in 1854, was quickly vetoed by President Franklin Pierce. Thus the most humanitarian of causes met political apathy and downright opposition.

Although he made no other public statements on woman's rights that I can find, we can learn from some of Lincoln's letters that, as in public matters, he regarded relations between the sexes as a subject of highest concern. There was in his view little or none of the romantic or archaic chivalry that embellished, even though tattered, the typical view from the plantation mansions which Mary Boykin Chesnut knew and described so well. He wrote to Mary Owens, whom he had been courting, on August 16, 1837, "I want in all cases to do right, and most particularly so, in all cases with women. I want, at this particular time, more than any thing else, to do right with you, and if I knew it would be doing right, as I rather suspect it would, to let you alone, I would do it." [12]

Perhaps this is the place to acknowledge that for Lincoln, as for many a man before his day and since, the problem of "doing right" with women had sexual and emotional complexities which troubled him as a young man even more deeply than doing right in any other matter, personal or political. What our modern slang might call his "sexual hangups" seem to have driven him out of the realm where reason—that "cold, calculating, unimpassioned reason" which he liked to think could solve political problems[13]—was able to provide either satisfaction or solution. But that is another story, which has not yet been adequately told, although the late Ruth Randall did as well as she could, and perhaps better than anyone else to date. Her *Mary Lincoln: Biography of a Marriage* is a model of what female historians have to do in order to counteract the prejudice, misunderstanding, and misrepresentation by even the well-intentioned male historians and biographers of practically every important woman in American history. Even the well-meaning male historian has all too often, at best, overlooked or neglected the real importance of what women did and said in the course of American history. It is the same story with black Americans. Frequently, not until black and female scholars have written it has their story begun to emerge in something like the texture that the future student should know for "how it was."

Not the least of Ruth Randall's achievements is her setting the record straight with the truth that females recorded but many male historians ignored or dismissed. Such is the testimony of the mulatto seamstress Elizabeth Keckley, one of Mary Lincoln's closest friends in Washington, and that of the abolitionist Jane Gray Swisshelm (whom not even Sandburg in his catchall *Abraham Lincoln: The War Years* could mention once). Jane Swisshelm and Elizabeth Keckley corroborate each other's accounts on one particular subject otherwise neglected; namely, that Mary Lincoln was well in advance of her husband on the need for freeing the slaves and on the essential nature of the war as a war to abolish slavery. It was likewise Mary Lincoln's friendship with abolitionist Senator Charles Sumner, her closest friendship with any important public figure or politician in Washington, which on occasion enabled the president to gain political footage he might not otherwise have gotten. As Sumner put it, "This is the first administration in which I have ever felt disposed to visit *the house* and I consider it a *privilege.*"[14]

One little known episode illustrates both a woman's impact on history and Lincoln's reliance on Sumner to get results.[15] The widow of gallant Maj. Lionel F. Booth, who fell along with most of the black troops he commanded at Fort Pillow on April 12, 1864, was impressed when she visited her husband's grave by the sad plight of the widows and orphans of the black troops. As ex-slaves most of these Union soldiers had never been permitted to marry, and hence their widows could not legally qualify as wives. When the doughty Mrs. Booth visited President Lincoln on May 19, 1864, and presented the case, he gave her a letter to Senator Sumner saying, "She makes a point, which I think very worthy of consideration which is, widows and children in *fact*, of colored soldiers who fall in our service, be placed in law, the same as if their marriages were legal, so that they can have the benefit of the provisions made the widows and orphans of white soldiers."[16] As a result, the bill then pending enactment by Congress was revised to provide just the equal treatment for black widows and children which Mrs. Booth went to Washington to ask the president to get for them.

Women played a much larger role in the Civil War than is recognized in either the general or the military histories. This is demonstrable to anyone who will look for the available but still inadequate accounts of the hosts of women who volunteered as nurses under the direction of the redoubtable Dorothea Dix, (appointed superintendent of women nurses, June 10, 1861) or under their own direction like Jane Gray Swisshelm, one of several independent souls who found it difficult to take Miss Dix's arbitrary discipline and went her own way in administering to the sick and wounded. When it came to organizing the sanitary fairs by which this volunteer work was chiefly funded, or the plight of freedmen alleviated, women bore the brunt.

In the rallies and meetings to encourage enlistment of soldiers and support the war effort in general, women played a major role. One of them, Anna E. Dickinson, Quaker abolitionist, was a legend in her own time as the most inspiring orator of the period. Her meteoric rise began with a speech accusing Gen. George B. McClellan of treason for his failure at the tragic Union defeat at Ball's Bluff. One of the early competent women employees of the federal government, (in the Philadelphia Mint) she was already a target for male abuse because of her vigorous championship of women's rights, and her denunciation of McClellan gave the excuse for her firing. Thereafter she took to the rostrum with a vengeance. Young and beautiful as well as vivid and violent in her oratory, she became the speaker most in demand at abolition and Union rallies. Nathaniel P. Willis dubbed her the American Joan of Arc, and John W. Forney in his administration newspaper the *Washington Chronicle* vowed that "Joan of Arc never was grander." In the beginning she was inclined to support Lincoln. What seemed to nearly all abolitionists to be his inadequate policy on emancipation, however, brought more and more denunciations of Lincoln's slowness. When she interviewed Lincoln on January 16, 1864, and told him his emancipation policy was not moving fast enough, he replied "'All I can say is, if the radicals want me to lead, let them get out of the way and let me lead.' . . . When he said that, I came out and remarked to a friend, 'I have spoken my last word to President Lincoln.'" But when Lincoln went to hear her lecture in the House of Representatives that night, he heard her allude somewhat more complimentarily to her feelings, when at his inauguration she had seen the "sudden sunburst out of clouds as Lincoln stepped forward to take his oath of office. Miss Dickinson interpreted it as a happy omen. 'The President,' wrote [Noah] Brooks, 'sat directly in front of the speaker, and from the reporters' gallery, behind her, I had caught his eye, soon after he sat down. When Miss Dickinson referred to the sunbeam, he looked up to me, involuntarily, and I thought his eyes were suffused with moisture. Perhaps they were, but the next day he said, "I wonder if Miss Dickinson saw me wink at you?"'" [17]

Few persons who differed with her had Lincoln's sense of humor, however, and her fall was no less meteoric than her rise. Though she continued to campaign vigorously and bitterly, not only for Negro rights but for woman's rights and mass education among other causes, newspaper editors responded with vituperation and invective that equaled or exceeded her own. She sued for libel and collected damages from New York newspapers that had repeatedly called her insane. Though this victory left her vindicated, it also marked her retreat from the public platform to live the life of a recluse until her death.

In Lincoln's dealings with forceful women such as Jane Swisshelm, Dorothea Dix, and Clara Barton, he seems a little better to have lived up to his early wish "to do right" by women. Perhaps it was because their work did not take them out of the male-approved female role of nurse and comforter of the sick and wounded. Hardly any of them failed to interview him, and some volunteered a piece of their mind. But one other woman was difficult for him to handle, Anna Ella Carroll of Maryland.

No other American woman or man of the nineteenth century was more politically oriented or better trained in the law than Anna Ella Carroll. Had she not been a woman, one scarcely can doubt that she would have achieved a distinguished career as a lawyer and/or public official. Born in 1815 she practically grew up in the library of her father, Thomas King Carroll, elected as a Jackson Democrat governor of Maryland in 1829. She was his favorite child and served as his private secretary. She made her own way thereafter as a professional woman—teaching, writing, and engaging in politics on behalf of the American, or Know-Nothing, party. Even more than her father, who had broken with the Roman Catholicism which nurtured most of the Maryland Carrolls, she became strenuously anti-Catholic, possibly because of the increasingly tight control of Democratic politics in Maryland by the influential Catholic slavocracy in collaboration with the Irish Catholic immigrants who were undercutting the native American laborers and craftsmen in Baltimore. In 1858 she helped Thomas H. Hicks get elected as a Know-Nothing governor of Maryland. With the election of Lincoln, she and Governor Hicks, along with many another Know-Nothing, became an important force in pursuading the critical border state of Maryland to hold fast to the Union. In the early months after Lincoln's inauguration, she produced two extremely well argued pamphlets—a Reply to Senator John C. Breckenridge's speech urging the border states to secede, and *The War Powers of the General Government*, both published in 1861. A third pamphlet published in 1862 was entitled *The Relation of the National Government to the Revolted Citizens Defined*. These influential publications articulated the theory upon which Lincoln acted, and stated the Union case better than any other writings except Lincoln's own.

These last two legal arguments were produced, according to Miss Carroll's own statements and acknowledged by Assistant Secretary of War Thomas A. Scott, under a verbal contract that she would be paid by the government for her expenses and labor. Scott had paid her out of his own pocket $1,250 for ten thousand extra copies of her *Reply to Breckenridge*. She was not paid anything further. Upon taking her claim to Lincoln for what she considered a reasonable amount of $50,000 to cover not merely her own labor over a period of two years, but the expense of travel on War Department business and the printing and distribution of the three pamphlets in the thousands, she was rebuffed by the president, who termed it "the most outrageous one ever made to any government, upon earth." Her reply was characteristic: "I remarked that, the difference between us, was in our views, upon the value of intellectual labor." [18]

Lincoln's rebuff is understandable, but scarcely justifiable, considering the pay for legal advice and opinion that he knew to be current among lawyers of the high caliber of Secretary Stanton, Attorney General Bates, and even himself, in highly important cases. Certainly, to quote Abigail Adams's comment to her husband already noted in a different context, he was "not very generous to the ladies," especially when this one had made it clear that she was not selling her patriotism, but her workmanship. It came also at a most crucially significant time, shortly after she had published on August 5, 1862, to quote the words of Lincoln's attorney general, Edward Bates, "your able and patriotic address of the 5th instant to your State which has equal relevancy to mine and all border States. I trust and believe its influence will go far to fill the quota now required without resort to a draft on the militia of the several States." Bates had been and continued to be her close friend, and doubtless sought to mollify her hurt feelings when he enclosed with his letter a note from Lincoln dated August 19, 1862, also thanking her for her address.[19]

Miss Carroll had a right to be indignant, since Thomas Scott and Edward Bates seem to have advised her that fifty thousand dollars would be a reasonable figure for her expenses and work, which was to continue as long as necessary. It likewise may have seemed to her especially ungracious of the president when she considered the fact that Lincoln had used her opinion as well as that of his attorney general (who had requested and submitted it along with his own) a year earlier when he phrased his reasons for suspending the writ of habeas corpus in Maryland.[20]

But hers is a long and complicated story of services often used and appreciated but unrewarded, and I cannot get into the further question of just how much recognition should go to her for making the reconnaissance and first forwarding to the War Department the essential recommendation and plan for Grant's invasion of the South up the Tennessee River. Professional historians have been even more ungenerous than Lincoln, for they have almost totally ignored her just claim, and left the writing of her biography to amateurs and novelists who perhaps go too far in seeking to redress her wrongful treatment. To quote Avery Craven: "By claiming too much the authors have injured rather than helped the reputation of a good lady who may have been somewhat neglected by historians."[21]

So far as Lincoln is concerned, however, I cannot give him very high marks for his treatment of either Miss Carroll or Miss Dickinson as equals. Brought up in what John Adams called "our masculine system," he did not treat any man who interviewed him or wrote to him (I think of Horace Greeley) with so little apparent respect for his intelligence in holding views at odds with those of the president of the United States. Perhaps reason, "cold, calculating, unimpassioned reason," which he could put to work on Greeley or Frederick Douglass as one man to another, somehow got mixed with other ingredients when Lincoln was confronted by an intellectual female, his equal in every respect, but of a different sex. The record is plain that Lincoln, his attorney general, and his War Department used Anna Ella Carroll almost completely, and though it was her own wish to be used, she should have been treated at least as well as a man would have been for equal service. Her full story needs yet to be told without either laudatory synthetics or the deprecatory male bias, which even in the best "professional" account as of this date seems to lean over backward to disallow her achievements; that is, the sketch of Anna Ella Carroll in *Notable American Women 1607– 1950*, which publication only belatedly and sometimes inadequately redresses the male bias of the *Dictionary of American Biography*.

I do not regard Lincoln's treatment of Jessie Benton Frémont as being in the same category as that of Anna Dickinson and Anna Carroll, for Jessie's husband, Gen. John C. Frémont, had sorely tried Lincoln's patience, and his wife insisted on injecting herself with singular vehemence into what should have remained the General's problem. Also, one must remember that her account of Lincoln's "sneering tone," when he remarked "You are quite a political female," gives no inkling of her own tone of address preceding the remark.[22] She made no effort to disguise her contempt for Lincoln, then or later, and the worst one can say is that Lincoln let her pull him down to her level of discourse. He simply lost his cool, as modern slang would put it.

Lincoln's personal relations with Negroes, more so than with women, were almost models of democratic correctness and friendly courtesy. Two instances among them are perhaps worthy of especial mention. As Mrs. Lincoln's closest personal female friend in Washington, the seamstress Elizabeth Keckley left her own account of how she knew the Lincolns at first hand, as friends as well as employers.[23] She was treated shabbily later on by Robert Todd Lincoln who wanted her book suppressed and who tried to prevent his mother from having anything to do with "Lizzie." Racist, male-biased newspapers were never worse than in their treatment of both Lincoln's widow and her Negro friend. But in spite of all, Mary Lincoln maintained and Elizabeth Keckley respected their friendship. President Lincoln's friendship was necessarily secondary to that of his wife, but it was no less personal and warmly equalitarian, insofar as their respective stations permitted.

Whenever I think of the Lincolns' personal relations with Negroes, I think that the clue to what Lincoln might have done, had his life been spared, in an effort to work out his plan of Reconstruction was best suggested in his letter to Gen. Nathaniel P. Banks, August 5, 1863. He hoped for Louisiana to seek "some practical system by which the two races could gradually live themselves out of their old relation to each other, and both come out better for the new."[24] The Lincolns had begun it personally and knew it worked.

With black William H. Johnson of Springfield, who accompanied Lincoln to the White House as personal servant, and of whom the newspaper reporter Henry Villard wrote, "although not exactly the most prominent, is yet the most useful member of the party,"[25] Lincoln's relationship was unique. Johnson served Lincoln with devotion until his death from smallpox, probably contracted from Lincoln himself on the return trip from Gettysburg in November, 1863. This story I have told at some length elsewhere,[26] but suffice it to say here that this relationship was courteous, democratic, and mutually serviceable, as Lincoln did for Johnson no less than Johnson did for him. For the whole story of Lincoln's personal and public relations with blacks the fine book by Benjamin F. Quarles, Lincoln and the Negro, should be read, but I wish to conclude with a summary of the relationship between President Lincoln and Frederick Douglass, certainly the greatest American Negro of the nineteenth century and perhaps one of the truly great men of any race in American history.

Douglass's early experience as a slave gave him the firsthand knowledge which his brilliant mind and literary style—developed, like Lincoln's, through self-education and practice—brought to the antislavery prose classic which he first published in 1845 under the title Narrative of the Life of Frederick Douglass, and revised in 1855 as My Bondage and My Freedom. Not only a truly great writer but also a gifted orator, Douglass took his place among the very top abolitionist orators, such as Wendell Phillips, and journalists, such as William Lloyd Garrison. The many times that racist newspapers and Democratic politicians singled him out for excoriation suggest that possibly only Garrison ranked higher as a recognized enemy of the then "establishment."

As might be expected, Douglass, like other abolitionists, welcomed Lincoln's election but followed the early course of his administration with little enthusiasm. He was, and continued to be, however, a more practical critic than the likes of Garrison and Phillips, and throughout the war was willing to compromise for the best he could get at the moment for the black people he represented. Always in advance of the president, who was, as Douglass recognized, the white man's president, unable to do more at any given time than white public opinion in the North would support, Douglass constantly worked to bring Lincoln toward the goal of emancipation and recognition of the Negro's possible contribution to the Union as a citizen and a soldier. Douglass did yeoman service in recruiting black soldiers, once Lincoln was brought to the point of ordering the establishment of black army units to fight as well as perform manual labor. He was dissatisfied, however, with the discrimination against and harsh treatment of black troops by army and civilian government officials, as well as alarmed by the particular Confederate savagery toward surrendering black Union soldiers demonstrated at every point of contact. He therefore sought an interview with the president sometime in July, 1863. This interview, as related by Douglass, was less than satisfactory, but he recognized Lincoln's carefully explained problem of doing as much as he could without alienating a large part of his public support, still predominantly prejudiced against the black man. One thing Douglass did get was the president's agreement that Negro soldiers should be promoted for good performance, and that he would "sign any commission to colored soldiers whom his Secretary of War commended."[27]

When Secretary Stanton was immediately approached by Douglass on this subject he found it difficult to say no, especially when Douglass offered to accept the first commission as an assistant on the staff of Gen. Lorenzo Thomas, adjutant general, to assist in further recruiting of black troops. Although promised, the commission never materialized, and Douglass refused to accept a civilian appointment at $100 per month and subsistence which was offered instead.

A second interview took place the next year, on either August 10 or August 19, 1864.[28] Douglass's own account in a manuscript dated August 29 relates that it dealt with Lincoln's idea for an unofficial agency to encourage and aid slaves to escape prior to conclusion of any peace negotiations.[29] Nothing came of this interview, but the account Judge Joseph T. Mills left of his own interview with Lincoln, immediately preceding Douglass's, contains a most interesting sidelight. As Mills's account moved toward conclusion, he told how "The President now in full flow of spirits, scattered his repartee in all directions. . . . Said I Mr President I was in your reception room to day. It was dark. . . . There in a corner I saw a man quietly reading who possessed a remarkable physiognomy. . . . I stood & stared at him. He raised his flashing eyes & caught me in the act. I was compelled to speak. Said I, Are you the President. No replied the stranger, I am Frederick Douglass. Now Mr. P. are you in favor of miscegenation. [Lincoln replied] That's a democratic mode of producing good Union men, & I dont propose to infringe on the patent."[30]

Two things interest me about this incident. First, Lincoln's total good humor in having Douglass, whose very striking, bearded mulatto face was not much darker than Lincoln's sallow bearded one, mistaken for himself. The second thing is not merely the aptness, but the widening circles of implication for speculation in his metaphorical answer. For although Lincoln's public pronouncements on miscegenation consistently stated his personal view that miscegenation was not for him, and that it was probably not for most, I believe he recognized it had been and would probably continue to be a principal concern between the two races, which individuals would have to meet as individuals. I have examined Lincoln's many statements on the subject, with the conclusion that one can infer, if he so chooses, and it has been assumed, that Lincoln thought miscegenation wrong, but in none do I find the categorical view clearly stated, and I remember that he could, and did when he wished, categorically state the right or the wrong of any matter or fact on moral, legal, or historical grounds.

Douglass's third interview with Lincoln came at the White House reception following the second inauguration. Such affairs were not for blacks, as Douglass knew, but he went anyway and was thrown out by two policemen. He sent a message to the president, and Lincoln summoned him in for an extended chat while the line of white handshakers waited. Douglass never questioned Lincoln's personal respect and genuine appreciation. He stated publicly of his earlier interviews that "the President of the United States received a black man at the White House just as one gentleman received another." Lincoln's democratic cordiality was reinforced by Sojourner Truth also. After the assassination, Douglass was deeply moved when Lincoln's widow sent him the president's walking stick with the word that Lincoln had once said he wished to present Douglass with some token of his regard. "Of all the numerous gifts he ever received—including objects from Daniel O'Connell, Elizabeth Cady Stanton, Lucretia Mott, Charles Sumner, and Queen Victoria—Douglass prized Lincoln's cane above all others."[31]

In after years, Douglass on two occasions gave his assessment of

Lincoln. The first was at the unveiling on April 14, 1876, of Thomas Ball's memorial sculpture, showing Lincoln holding in his right hand the Emancipation Proclamation with his left poised above a kneeling slave. The execution of this monument had been paid for by subscription from Negroes. Douglass's speech remains today, the best understanding and assessment of Lincoln by any of his contemporaries, white or black. It gives the measure of Lincoln's greatness by a mind no less great and fully aware of the degree to which personal experience and even prejudice goes into every man's character, white or black. I would recommend its reading in full by every student, white or black, who would pass a judgment on Lincoln, but I can quote it only in brief part:

He was pre-eminently the white man's President, entirely devoted to the welfare of white men. He was ready and willing at any time during the first years of his administration to deny, postpone, and sacrifice the rights of humanity in the colored people to promote the welfare of the white people of this country. . . . The race to which we belong were not the special objects of his consideration. Knowing this, I concede to you, my white fellow-citizens, a pre-eminence in this worship at once full and supreme. . . . You are the children of Abraham Lincoln. We are at best his step-children; children by adoption, children by forces of circumstances and necessity. To you it especially belongs to sound his praises. . . . But . . . while Abraham Lincoln saved for you a country, he delivered us from a bondage, according to Jefferson, one hour of which was worse than ages of the oppression your fathers rose in rebellion to oppose.

But . . . taking him for all in all, measuring the tremendous magnitude of the work before him, considering the necessary means to ends, and surveying the end from the beginning, infinite wisdom has seldom sent any man into the world better fitted for his mission than Abraham Lincoln.[32]

Douglass's second assessment, somewhat more mellow, was written ten years later as a contribution to a collection of reminiscences about Lincoln. In it Douglass said: "In all my interviews with Mr. Lincoln I was impressed with his entire freedom from popular prejudice against the colored race. He was the first great man that I talked with in the United States freely, who in no single instance reminded me of the differences between himself and myself, of the difference of color."[33]

In retrospect, it is sad to recall how so many noble women and brave men, who had struggled for years both to abolish slavery and to achieve equal rights for women, fell into disagreement once the Civil War was finished over whether priority should go to Negro suffrage or woman suffrage; and how Douglass, so long a champion of both, felt he must give priority to his race and, for practical reasons, to alignment with the Republican party. This left Elizabeth Cady Stanton, Susan B. Anthony, and other true reformers to struggle on in their Equal Rights Association and, later, the National Woman Suffrage Association, not only without aid, but with actual opposition from some of their former black collaborators. Does one wonder that it took fifty years after the Fifteenth Amendment, which might have given suffrage to women no less than blacks by the simple insertion of a few words, before the Nineteenth Amendment would be passed and ratified? And does one wonder whether or whenever the Equal Rights Amendment of our day will be ratified?

Two hundred years is a long time, but perhaps not long enough for Americans to learn to read the Declaration's immortal proposition as Lincoln read it, and ask with him "Where are we? And where are we going?" Too many Americans are perhaps like the little boy who explained his report card by saying, "I'm a slow reader because I don't want to read." Our progress has been slow, more than slow, reluctant, to recognize that the self-evident truth meant more than even Thomas Jefferson or John Adams could have guessed. But let us honor both Jefferson and Lincoln for having avowed that "stumbling block" of all tyranny and oppression.

PART 2

**Lincoln and the
Idea of Progress**

FOUR
The Right to Rise

G. S. BORITT

*To [secure] to each labourer the whole product of his labour, or as
nearly as possible, is a most worthy object of any good government.
But then the question arises, how can a government best, effect this?
In our own country, in it's present condition. . . .*—From fragments
of a tariff discussion, c. 1847

*I hold the value of life is to improve one's condition. Whatever is
calculated to advance the condition of the honest, struggling labor-
ing man, so far as my judgment will enable me to judge of a correct
thing, I am for that thing.*—From speech to Germans at Cincinnati,
Ohio, 1861

Anno Domini 1865. Oak Ridge Cemetery, Springfield, Illinois. Bishop Matthew Simpson was delivering the funeral sermon. He quoted
the deceased in words of deep conviction, words that spoke of a
great work to be done. They conjured up the specter of an evil in the
land: "Broken by it, I, too, may be; bow to it I never will. The *probability* that we may fall in the struggle *ought not* to deter us from the
support of a cause we believe to be just. It *shall not* deter me."

The declaration was that of young Abraham Lincoln on the day
after Christmas, 1839. The bishop interpreted his text in a way and
with an authority that seemed wholly natural to the mourning nation. Here was the testament of the beloved martyr dedicating himself in his youth to the great struggle of his life against the Slave
Power.

Bishop Simpson quoted Lincoln accurately. He had unearthed a
long-lost speech that would soon be lost again. But he did make one
error. Lincoln's speech had said nothing about slavery. Its subject
was banking.[1]

If it is a little surprising to associate Lincoln with banks, that is a
reflection upon the common image of him, shared by many scholars

57

and laymen. On careful examination, however, the surprise should evaporate. In more than three decades of public life Lincoln probably talked more about economics, to use the term broadly, than any other issue, slavery included.[2] The bulk of his discussions with an economic focus preceded the period of his fame and hence went unrecorded. But the main lines of his thinking survive, as do, frequently, details. Just as significantly, Lincoln's noneconomic speeches and writings often brimmed with economic implications. Historians have heretofore largely avoided this rich material—why, cannot be explained here in brief. By focusing on it, however, I hope to suggest a hypothesis about a substantially new, and vigorous image of Lincoln.

The key to his economic persuasion was an intense and continually developing commitment to the ideal that all men should receive a full, good, and ever-increasing reward for their labors so that they might have the opportunity to rise in life. For the son of obscure backwoods parents—who in time rose to the White House—this commitment was also a personal one. And this, Lincoln's American Dream, became a central theme throughout his entire political life.

In intellectual terms the theme grew from a combination of economic orientation and sympathy for what Lincoln called "the many poor," but what we should simply label "the many," to what might be seen by the 1850s as a full-blown ideology. During the first and longer part of his public life it found expression through the support of governmental policies that primarily aimed at economic development (however rudimentarily he, and his age, understood this modern concept). Like thousands of others, Lincoln grasped the fact that such development improved the chances of "the many" to improve their lives.

Thus in 1830, Lincoln's first verifiable speech called for improving the transportation system of Illinois—"internal improvements" as Americans of the time spoke of it. Two years later he entered politics on a platform of such improvement. Then, in1837, his first fully published address discussed banking in Illinois. In 1840 his first political pamphlet focused on banking on the national scene and won him his first notice in Washington. In 1847 his first address to a national audience, too, took political economy—internal improvements again —for its subject.[3] These "firsts" carried both symbolic and strategic meanings and reveal much about him and his age. But more important, in between these milestones, and for years after, Lincoln made economics the most substantial element of his campaigning, legislative labors, and private studies outside, and not infrequently inside, his legal practice.

Illinois's brave (although often somewhat unfairly described as foolish) attempt to join the transportation revolution of the 1830s is Lincoln's best-known economic involvement. On this, as on most other economic policies, his devotion to developmental, right to rise economics remained essentially unchanged over a lifetime. It began with such things as the young state legislator's demand for building a bridge at New Salem on the Sangamon and ended with the federal legislation for building the Pacific Railroad.

Internal improvement, however, is one of the few Lincolnian connections with economics to receive at least some mildly focused scrutiny. His often more intimate ties with hosts of related matters tend to be ignored, passed over lightly, or, when dealt with, generally analyzed in almost exclusively political, and thus to a degree misleading, terms. An early, telling Lincoln action toward banks provides a nice illustration of this.

Most Lincoln students are familiar with the story of his leap from the window of Springfield's Second Presbyterian Church where the Illinois House of Representatives was meeting in 1840. Nominally the issue at stake was adjournment. The Democratic majority desired it; Lincoln and his fellow Whigs hoped to block it by boycotting sessions and preventing the presence of a quorum. Lincoln and a few followers, however, remained in attendance to keep an eye on the proceedings which at the crucial moment included the sergeant at arms fetching delinquent solons back into the church by force. What followed was described with great relish by the press of the time and recited by historians since:

Mr. Lincoln . . . who appeared to enjoy the embarrassment of the House, suddenly looked very grave after the Speaker announced that a quorum was present. The conspiracy having failed, Mr. Lincoln, came under great excitement, and having attempted and failed to get out at the door, very unceremoniously raised the window and jumped out, followed by one or two other members. This gymnastic performance of Mr. Lincoln and his flying brethren did not occur until after they had voted and consequently the House did not interfere with their extraordinary feat. We have not learned whether these flying members got hurt in the adventure, and we think it probable that at least one of them came off without damage, as it was noticed that his legs reached nearly from the window to the ground! . . . We learn that a resolution will probably be introduced into the House this week to inquire into the expedience of raising the State House one story higher . . . so as to prevent members from jumping out windows! If such a resolution passes, Mr. Lincoln in future will have to climb down the spout.

The virtue of narrating the honorable gentleman's action this way is obvious, and stressing the politicking has a certain validity. But it does in the end obscure the ultimate meaning of Lincoln's action. For he acted in such an unorthodox fashion in a desperate attempt to defend the banking system of Illinois against what he believed to be politically prejudiced and economically ignorant attacks.

Lincoln won many such battles but the Springfield defenestration failed. The adjournment of the legislature in turn meant that the State Bank of Illinois which, like most other banks in the nation, had suspended specie payment because of the depression, was forced to resume payment, that is to redeem its paper money in silver and gold. Since in the Midwest Illinois acted alone in allowing redemption, the exaggerated demand of the whole region for specie fell upon her. In a few weeks nearly a half a million dollars were drained from the state—an exceedingly large sum for that time and place. When at last the legislators came around to Lincoln's way of looking at things, the damage had been done. They thus deserve part of the blame for the collapse of the state's banking system within a year. Lincoln's hasty departure through the church window aimed at preventing that collapse.[4]

Fighting for long years the unpopular battle for banking, Lincoln insisted that he was above all fighting for the "farmer and mechanic."[5] In part, he thus met the requirements of American politics. In part, however, he also gave voice to the prime element of a developing economic persuasion. The fact was that for the man who would rise, for the nation that would rise, banks were necessary.

Lincoln's Whiggish economics (for on the whole they were such even if their underlying world view was broadly American) went hand in hand with the hope that a wide recognition of their benefits would provide political preferment. His hopes for America and his Whig, and later Republican, attachments were firmly intertwined. Yet his willingness to uphold economic measures that were unpopular in Illinois deserves repeated emphasis. And lest we make too much of his partisan loyalties and party regularity, we should note that for more than a decade and a half he failed to champion the noneconomic principles of his Whig party—the single term presidency, for example, or opposition to immigrants, or to a tight political organization. In contrast he upheld his own version of the Whig economic vision even in private, whether writing to a political opponent about taxes or to his kinsman about the way to rise in life.[6]

Lincoln supported banking, above all, for the same reason he supported a whole set of related economic policies. Even the skeletal records of his early career speak to us of a vision of American progress, a dream of national improvement in the fullest sense of the term. He worked to build up the nation, he said, to cultivate it, "making it a garden." The "garden," of course, would be commercial and industrial as well as agricultural, and would secure for all the opportunity for full, fair, and growing "reward of their labors."[7] I am quoting here Lincolnian words that carried the deepest meaning for him throughout his life and were at the heart of his fully formed ideology.

Lincoln's intelligent interest in the banking question began in New Salem. (Three decades later as president he played a crucial—and by historians almost totally ignored—part in pushing Congress to adopt a national banking system.)[8] Fiscal matters, especially taxation, also drew his interest early. As a freshman representative in the Illinois House, for example, he demanded tax privileges for new settlers who had to start at the bottom—doing so in a minority of six against forty-one nays. A few years later he sought tax breaks for those who would plant forests on the treeless prairie. All along he groped in the direction of what our century calls progressive taxation. As president he signed such legislation into law.[9]

On the specific issue of industrialization, and the policy most tied to it, tariff protection, not a single Lincoln speech is extant. Yet if all he had said on the subject came down to us, that alone would have occupied perhaps two volumes of his *Collected Works*. As it is, we have fragments, such as Lincoln singing of the blight of an agrarian triumph: "All is cold and still as death—no [sm]oke rises, no furnace roars, no anvil rings." And on this question he became sufficiently learned (including reading political economists) to adopt the most avant-garde argument of his time, as developed by Henry Carey.[10]

His support of industry notwithstanding, Lincoln had a commitment to the small independent producer that dominated his America, and to the extent his economic views have been noticed—by Richard Hofstadter and a few others—this has been stressed. What therefore needs emphasis here is that Lincoln's commitment went

hand in hand with an understanding attitude toward the concentra-
tion of capital, the factory system, and, to balance these, an early,
firm commitment to labor unions. In the process of promoting railroad building in Illinois, for example, Lincoln gladly predicted—in
the 1840s—the movement toward giant corporations which only
came to characterize the industry after the Civil War. In the same
breath it should be mentioned that as president he pioneered what
we call "jawboning"—he used the executive power to coerce railroads into reducing freight charges. And he declared to a delegation
of striking workers that "I know that in almost every case of strikes,
the men have just cause for complaint." These, and other of his in-
sights and actions were, and long remained, unmatched by other
occupants of the White House.[11]

The significant point about Lincoln's commitment to the small,
independent producer is that it stemmed much more from Whig-
Republican economics than Jeffersonian-Democratic sociopolitical
reasoning. Thus his small producer embodied both the right to rise
and ever greater productivity and economic development. The two
indeed were identified so fully in his mind that we cannot say which
was more important to him. This in turn implies a substantial potential to accept economically inspired social change (leading away
from the independent producer) so long as the road to opportunity
remained open.

There is no need here to analyze, much less catalog, every aspect
of Lincoln's economic views. But before we come to slavery and war
one more topic should be considered: his neglect of agriculture and
his indifference to the nation's rapid westward expansion. His economic outlook helped shape his lack of enthusiasm toward expansionism for it bespoke an inward-looking orientation, characteristic
of many Whigs: a desire for internal instead of external development. Perhaps Lincoln was not as much against territorial expansion
per se, as he was in favor of concentrating the nation's energies within the country, making it a "garden." Rightly or wrongly, he refused
to go along with the majority of his countrymen and equate geographical with social mobility.[12]

Lincoln's opposition to manifest destiny went along with a blurred
stance on public land policies, although he did not toe a party line.
He showed little interest in the subject, indeed in anything agricultural, above all, because advancement was so important but working
the soil hardly the best road to it—whether for the individual or the

nation. He had grown up in the Arcady his fellow Americans vener-
ated, but had no illusions about it. His campaigning in 1840 gave a
poignant illustration of his attitudes. While the nation sang the jolly
rhyme "But we'll have a ploughman/President of the Cincinnatus
line," and while his Whig brethren became intoxicated with log
cabins and hard cider, Lincoln spoke soberly of the virtues of centralized banking. He never changed his priorities.[13]

Party politicking aside, Lincoln could sustain such a stance with
much immunity, in part because his message was attractive to many,
including farmers. Country lawyer that he was, he knew, better than
Emerson did, that the "Man With the Hoe" was "covetous of his
dollar." He presented his Whiggish economic policies as opening
the road of advancement to the farmer as well as to others. And over
the long run, at least in economic terms, he was right.

Lincoln's success with his predominantly farming constituency
(whether in Illinois or in the White House) stemmed also from great
political ability that was reinforced by his sincerity and his appearance and ways. He seemed like a man of the soil with manure on his
boots, even if the manure was not there. When accused of siding
with the aristocracy, he could ward off the charge rudely. In one
debate when his opponent warmed up to such a haranguing performance, Lincoln ripped open the good tribune's coat to reveal an
opulent gentleman with ruffled shirt, vest, and gold chain. The people roared. Then Lincoln reminisced about the times when he had
worked for eight dollars a month and about the single pair of buckskin breeches he had to his name: "Now if you know the nature of
buckskin when wet and dried by the sun, it will shrink; and my
breeches kept shrinking until they left several inches of my legs bare
between the tops of my socks and the lower part of my breeches; and
whilst I was growing taller they were becoming shorter, and so much
tighter that they left a blue streak around my legs that can be seen
to this day. If you call this aristocracy I plead guilty to the charge."[14]
There were not many who could doubt where Lincoln's allegiance
lay. He was of the people, the common men whom Lincoln said God
loved so and made so many of.[15]

And how does slavery fit into the picture sketched out here? The
answer is—centrally. Slavery, the lethal cancer, that Lincoln (blind-
ly and perhaps to a degree self-servingly) assumed to be on its way to
slow cure and dissolution through much of his political life, was
proved by the passage of the Kansas-Nebraska Act to be thriving and

aggressive. It became clear that no amount of improvement legislation could build the American Dream if the whole nation became a slave society. To put up an effective front against slavery, a Whig-Democratic coalition had to be created. The principal price of the new alliance was submerging the economic differences between the two old parties.[16] Lincoln was willing to pay that price because of his sharp perception of both the moral and the practical realities of the 1850s.

In his mind the roles of slavery and economics were thus reversed. Economics provided the central motif of Lincoln's career before 1854; antislavery was pushed in the background, its triumph placed at a distant day. After 1854, antislavery became Lincoln's immediate goal, and the economic policies that he continued to esteem highly (and work for when possible) he relegated to the background and to a future triumph. Political expediency had much to do with both the first and second compromises of his beliefs. His underlying assumptions, however, his moral underpinnings, remained unchanged. Indeed, when Lincoln actively embraced the antislavery cause, he raised his Dream to its highest plane. The challenge of this moral ascent, in turn, inspired him to enunciate more clearly and more beautifully than ever before the ideals he stood for.

The "central idea" of America was equality, Lincoln noted in 1856, taking his stand squarely on the Declaration of Independence. Whether his historical judgment was accurate is open to question. But we can be certain that the meaning he gave to Jefferson's words was scarcely identical with Jefferson's own. Whatever equality meant to the Virginian and his age, Lincoln crowned the work of the Jacksonian generation by extending its meaning to equality of opportunity to get ahead in life. This was his "central idea." One may dare to suggest that this is one of the most important metamorphoses of an idea in American history.[17]

In the 1850s, Lincoln defined again and again his central idea as "the principle that clears the path for all—gives hope to all—and, by consequence, enterprize, and industry to all." Hofstadter was therefore correct in concluding that Lincoln's most "vital test" of democracy was economic. In the absence of previous research, he could not add that this was the fruit of the Illinoisan's economic orientation and of the orientation of the age which spawned him and which eagerly accepted this new definition of equality.[18]

Slavery subverted the American Dream. It did so in myriad ways, but perhaps most importantly, by denying blacks the right to rise, slavery endangered that right for all. Thus he slowly found his way to the view that blacks, too, must be allowed to rise as high as their ability could take them. "I want every man to have a chance," he said. "And I believe a black man is entitled to it—in which he can better his condition—when he may look forward and hope to be a hired laborer this year and the next, work for himself afterward, and finally to hire men to work for him! That is the true system." This nation has been struggling to live up to that ideal since.[19]

When war came Lincoln once again could give attention to some economic policies. He not only helped set the tone, but in some cases —perhaps most importantly banking—he made crucial contributions to the economic blueprint that Congress created for modern America. More revealing, however, is the way his economic orientation strongly colored and at times determined his antislavery and war stance—down to his attempts to make peace, or forge military strategy. Believing honest wages to be the key to advancement for the poor, he projected a fair wage relationship as the heart of his policies toward the former slaves. And with the aid of the freedmen, he effectively killed the deep (but economically disastrous) American hope for colonizing blacks abroad.[20]

In searching for peace and reunion, his best, certainly most extensive, argument ("Physically speaking, we cannot separate") was largely economic.[21] A major component of his numerous peace feelers and reconstruction schemes was an appeal to the economic interests of the Rebels. He assumed somewhat naïvely (and in a way that can now be labeled "typically American") that the South could be seduced into peace via materialist enticement. This assumption largely explains in no small part the absurdly vast amount of time he devoted to the problems of trading with the Confederacy, especially in cotton. The same is true of his secret feelers about the federal takeover of the Confederate war debt (obliquely attacked in the Wade-Davis Manifesto), his persistent offers for large scale compensation for slaves, what Kenneth M. Stampp saw fit to call Lincoln's "sabotage" of congressional laws of confiscation, perhaps even the unrealistic presidential demand that the Pacific Railroad be built on the five feet gauge used primarily in the South.[22]

The large economic ingredient in his plans for reunification and peacemaking was quite matched in his war making. The blockade, his emphasis on the military importance of railroads and new weapons, and, in part, his insistence on the strategic significance of the black troops, or the Mississippi Valley, provide straightforward illustrations of this ingredient. More subtle is the link between his economic persuasion and the strategic innovations that permit historians to speak of Lincoln's military genius.[23] Thus, the man who in the 1840s demanded from Congress a centralized and coordinated plan of national improvements, in the 1860s made like demands upon his generals for centralization of authority and coordination of plans. And so the Union's unified command system and its central, overall plan of strategy were born. Similarly, Lincoln's decisive championship of cordon offense (advancing on the enemy on every front, thus pitting all the Northern resources against all the Southern ones) stemmed primarily from his conviction that economic might, more than anything else excepting morale, would determine the outcome of the war. This oft attested conviction was also the fundamental catalyst of his recognition that the objective of the Union forces should be not the conquest of territories but the destruction of opposing armies, the destruction of "the most important branch of . . . resources": men.[24] And scholars agree, this recognition played a pivotal role in the Union victory.

Perhaps the most unsettling facet of Lincoln's military policy was the drastic rate at which federal commanders were replaced. On the eastern front, for example, in a period of two years he removed the general in charge an unprecedented seven times. Military historians often criticized him, harshly, for failing to support his commanders in defeat. Without engaging in the details of this controversy, we should note that Lincoln's actions reflected a core aspect of his economic outlook which under the pressure of war became extreme: He conducted a ruthless campaign of pushing the successful of the lower ranks to the fore. And his view that in the Civil War one side stood for the "open field" for all, and the other against it, thus received more than symbolic corroboration. In the Confederacy the men who held the chief commands early in the war were there when Appomattox came. Even if Jefferson Davis made a relatively fortunate initial selection of top generals, it is startling to note that the one exception to the above was the gallant Albert Sidney Johnston. And he was dead. In contrast, there was not a single general commanding a main army in the Union service of 1865 who had held high command at the beginning of the struggle. In this respect, Lincoln's American Dream had triumphed on the battlefield, too.

Recognizing the all-important role he assigned to the right to rise is not to diminish his devotion to other manifestations of democracy. Indeed these tended to become interchangeable in his utterances, particularly toward the end of the war. It hardly need be said that he was devoted to the Union, liberty, political democracy, and the importance of the American example to the world. But all these concepts, vital as they were, carried a certain aura of abstraction about them by his day, excepting perhaps the last few years of his life. His more down-to-earth, deep commitment to social order, in turn, was much more contravened than upheld by his decision to "accept war" in 1861. In contrast, the right of each man to the product of his labor, the right to rise, was almost palpably real, material—something ordinary people could fully understand and identify with. And his devotion to this right (which he correctly linked to economic development) provides the strongest thread of his life, that runs from New Salem through Washington.

If one is satisfied with pointing to an occasional early Lincoln utterance about political democracy and tying this to his eloquent presidential statements on the subject, it is possible to establish a certain ideological continuity between the politician of Illinois and the later statesman of world significance. If one is satisfied with pointing to some early Lincoln utterances, even some speeches, about moderation, law, order, and community and finding this continuous strain in the mature man, once again a continuity can be developed.

If one is satisfied with concentrating on the presidential years alone, one might find Lincoln's central message as did such disparate men as Alexander Stephens, Walt Whitman—and most Americans since—in a religious devotion to the Union. But if we scrutinize Lincoln's life as a whole, take stock both quantitatively and qualitatively, and thus see those final crowning years of conflict in the perspective sketched out here, we should speak—awkward as this is —about Lincoln's War for the American Dream.

The Union to him was not an end but a means. It was to be upheld so long as it upheld "that thing for which the Union itself was made." The Union was the ship, he explained, and the American Dream its cargo: "the prosperity and the liberties of the people." And "so long as the ship can be saved, with the cargo," he added, "it should never be abandoned."

Without the ship the cargo would go down and therefore it was senseless to emphasize a distinction between the two. Yet this imagery implied that had there been another equally seaworthy ship available, Lincoln might have been satisfied with transferring the cargo. But there was no other ship, the idea itself was beyond the realm of his practical thought. And so there had to be a war, to save the ship, yes, but to save the ship so that the cargo could be saved.[25]

This distinction, however unimportant it might have appeared at the time, held fateful meaning. The idea of the Union is essentially national, that of the Dream is universal. One view prizes the Civil War, to quote Francis Lieber, as "a war for nationality." It makes Lincoln into "the Great Nationalist" of the modern historians, a man who had a religious faith in the Union. The other cherishes him as an American Moses or Christ, one who spoke to mankind.[26]

At the same time, paradoxically, the first view denies the uniqueness of the United States. It values Lincoln as a New World counterpart of Cavour and Bismarck whose highest goal, to use the German's expression, was *"staatsbildung."* Without gainsaying the achievements of the Europeans, we must note that their degenerate twentieth-century descendants in the worship of the nation as an end in itself were Hitler and Mussolini. In contrast, Lincoln's Dream helped lead America to the nationalism of Theodore Roosevelt, Woodrow Wilson, and Franklin Delano Roosevelt.

Early in 1861, on his way to Washington, Lincoln spoke in Trenton, New Jersey, about the revolutionary war and the battle there in which Washington defeated the Hessians. His thoughts went back to his first childhood readings in history:

You all know . . . how these early impressions last longer than any others. I recollect thinking then, boy even though I was, that there must have been *something more* than common that those men struggled for. I am exceedingly anxious that *that thing* which they struggled for; *that something* even more than National Independence; *that something* that held out a great promise to all the people of the world to all time to come; I am exceedingly anxious that this Union, the Constitution, and the liberties of the people shall be perpetuated in accordance with *the original idea* for which that struggle was made, and I shall be most happy indeed if I shall be an humble instrument in the hands of the Almighty, and of this, his almost chosen people, for perpetuating *the object* of that great struggle.

It was perhaps the emotions born out of the remembrance of his own beginnings, that so possessed Lincoln's mind that he did not then explicitly define "*that something,*" "*the original idea*" of America, which he believed the nation's founders had already struggled for. Or perhaps it was the fault of the *New York Tribune* reporter that the president-elect's reflections in Trenton remained incomplete.

A day later, however, speaking in Independence Hall, at Philadelphia, Lincoln continued his revolutionary theme. He still spoke "with deep emotion," and now the press reported his completed thought: "It was that which gave promise that in due time the weights should be lifted from the shoulders of all men, and that *all* should have an equal chance." [27]

One suspects that remembering "way back," Lincoln exaggerated the clarity of his youthful ideas. Nevertheless, their seeds must have been there early, in the "earliest days of my being able to read," as he recalled. Indeed, for a moment, we must reach beyond these early days, to a toddler in Kentucky.

It was corn-planting time in the valley where the Lincolns made their home. Children had to be taught to work very young. Little Abe was beginning his lessons, walking behind his father, dropping pumpkin seeds into the hills made by Thomas's crude hoe. Two seeds in every second hill, in every second row. Then the Sabbath came and with it a great cloudburst up on the hills above them. It did not rain in their valley but the water came swirling down from the hills, washing away corn, pumpkin, and topsoil. The fruit of their labor was lost. This was the earliest memory, earliest pain, the grown man Lincoln could recall. Almost half a century later he told another Kentuckian, Cassius Clay: "I always thought that the man who made the corn should eat the corn." [28]

This then is a story of Lincoln. It had all begun with a poor boy's conviction—in a time and at a place which nurtured such convictions—that a man should receive the full fruit of his labor so that he might get ahead in life. The conviction matured slowly, over decades. And as Lincoln stood on the threshold of the White House, his conviction had become unshakable. The United States had to be saved *with* the Dream. "If this country cannot be saved without giving up that principle," he declared, "I would rather be assassinated." [29]

As the Civil War reached its climax and end, the president's concept of the American Dream also reached its ultimate heights. In the spring of 1865 he summed up for a final time the Rebel cause, as he saw it: "It may seem strange that any men should dare to ask a just God's assistance in wringing their bread from the sweat of other men's faces." But he added now: "let us judge not that we be not judged." Even for one of his legendary fortitude the "nation's wounds," and those of the men who had "borne the battle, and . . . his widow, and his orphan," proved too much to endure by reason alone. As his years of trial were about to end, he turned for support from a central idea that was the law of man, perhaps the law of nature, to that same idea as the law of God. Not surprisingly, for such is the way of man, Lincoln had found that the purpose of his Maker were like his own purposes.

"Fondly do we hope—fervently do we pray," he told his countrymen, "that this mighty scourge of war may speedily pass away. Yet, if God wills that it continue, until all the wealth piled by the bondman's two hundred and fifty years of unrequited toil shall be sunk, and until every drop of blood drawn with the lash, shall be paid by another drawn with the sword, as was said three thousand years ago, so still it must be said 'the judgments of the Lord, are true and righteous altogether.'"

Unrequited toil, unearned and bloodstained wealth: war as judgment. The denial of the Dream was to be expiated. The extorted labor of two and a half centuries had to be paid for. Lincoln's American Dream had become the will of God.[30]

FIVE
The Apostle of Progress

NORMAN A. GRAEBNER

During his campaign for the Republican nomination in September, 1859, Abraham Lincoln addressed a large Indianapolis audience. It was, he admitted, his first major address in Indiana. It seemed a proper occasion to recall his early life in Spencer County near the Ohio in southwest Indiana. "There was an unbroken wilderness there then," he said, "and an axe was put in [my] hand; and with the trees and logs and grubs [I] fought until [I] reached [my] twentieth year."[1] From that Indiana wilderness he soon entered another, equally remote and perhaps even more unsettled, the Sangamon frontier west of Decatur, Macon County, in central Illinois. On February 11, 1861, President-Elect Lincoln, after brief stops at Tolono and Danville, Illinois, addressed a huge throng at the Lafayette, Indiana, railroad station. He began his remarks with this observation: "We have seen great changes within the recollection of some of us who are the older. When I first came to the west, some 44 or 45 years ago, at sundown you had completed a journey of some 30 miles which you had commenced at sunrise, and thought you had done well. Now only six hours have elapsed since I left my home in Illinois where I was surrounded by a large concourse of my fellow citizens, almost all of whom I could recognize, and I find myself far from home surrounded by the thousands I now see before me, who are strangers to me."[2]

The Old Northwest had changed. Those three decades which spanned Lincoln's life in the Sangamon country witnessed no less than a demographic and economic revolution in Illinois. The state had emerged from a wilderness of rivers and roads, farms and villages, to a highly developed region of railroads and commerce, industry, and cities of immense activity. Lincoln had lived through one of the most dynamic and changeful eras in history. Was he mindful of these changes? Did he play a role in effecting them? If growth to him meant progress, how did he define it?

Even as a youth in Indiana, Lincoln identified emotionally with that progressive frontier element which preferred commerce and movement to farming. Early he hoped to escape the narrow life of the woods by obtaining a position on an Ohio River steamboat. He resisted that urge, but in 1828, in company with another young man, he successfully guided a flatboat of produce to New Orleans.[3] Even as Lincoln, two years later, accompanied his family to the new settlements along the north fork of the Sangamon, he had no intention of remaining long on the farm. Indeed, he reentered the frontier world of commerce as early as the spring of 1831 when Denton Offutt, a merchant of varied interests, invited him to take another flatboat and cargo to New Orleans.

Melting snows made the Sangamon appear navigable when Lincoln, with two companions, traveled to the designated rendezvous of Springfield and there met Offutt at Elliott's Tavern. Springfield had emerged in the 1820s as the seat of Sangamon County, but beyond that distinction it was scarcely a promising community. At Springfield, Lincoln and his associates built a flatboat and descended the Sangamon to New Salem where the boat became lodged on the new village's mill dam. Lincoln, to Offutt's admiration, dislodged the boat and continued downstream to his destination. That summer he returned home briefly but left again in August. Offutt and New Salem brought Lincoln permanently into the world of trade and commerce without providing either the opportunity or the incentive to turn him into a frontier entrepreneur. Lincoln remained poor. Unlike many ambitious, enterprising, and often visionary pioneers, Lincoln was not a speculator who in the affluent thirties spent his time laying out townsites and peddling real estate. Still from the beginning he shared the Whiggish approach to frontier development which focused on improved transportation with its resultant growth of population and commerce, if not land values.

Lincoln's immediate concern for improved commerce centered on the Sangamon. To his delight he discovered in the *Sangamo Journal* of January 26, 1832, that a Cincinnati boat captain planned to ascend the Sangamon to Springfield when the western rivers became clear of ice. Later Lincoln joined the group that traveled to Beardstown on the Illinois to welcome the "splendid upper-cabin steamer," *Talisman*. Lincoln piloted the steamer successfully to the Springfield wharf as the city celebrated the long-awaited event which proved that it was no longer a mere inland town. But the *Talisman* soon left and never returned. Neither the state nor the nation ever removed the snags from the Sangamon River.[4]

Illinois in 1830 had reached a population of 157,000. Its settlements were limited to the wooded borders of the leading watercourses. North and east of Peoria the state remained a wilderness, for its wide prairies held little attraction for the early settlers. Moreover, the prairies lay too far from navigable streams to permit successful commercial farming. Many doubted that the prairies would ever be occupied.[5] Even much of the Sangamon country lacked the needed transportation to provide an expanding future. Lincoln did not reject immediately the notion that the Sangamon would one day carry the region's commerce, but he quickly placed his faith in other modes of conveyance. His contribution to their development began quickly as he turned from a life of trade to one of politics and law.

Lincoln entered his first race for the state legislature in 1832 as a Henry Clay Whig, devoted to a program of internal improvements, but one that would not exceed the financial limits of those who undertook it. Addressing the people of Sangamon County on March 9, he declared:

Time and experience have verified to a demonstration, the public utility of internal improvements. That the poorest and most thinly populated countries would be greatly benefitted by the opening of good roads, and in the clearing of navigable streams within their limits, is what no person will deny. And yet it is folly to undertake works of this or any other kind, without first knowing that we are able to finish them—as half finished work generally proves to be labor lost. There cannot justly be any objection to having rail roads and canals, any more than to other good things, provided they cost nothing. The only objection is to paying for them; and the objection to paying arises from the want of ability to pay.[6]

Lincoln reminded the citizens of Sangamon County that their region required better communication if it would export more profitably its surplus products and import more readily whatever manufactured goods it found necessary. Already, noted Lincoln, a public meeting at Jacksonville to the west of Springfield had considered the possibility of constructing a railroad from some convenient location on the Illinois through Jacksonville to Springfield. Lincoln praised the project, for the railroad, he said, "is a never failing source of communication, between places of business remotely situated from each other. Upon the rail road the regular progress of commercial intercourse is not interrupted by either high or low water, or freezing weather, which are the principal difficulties that render our future hopes of water communication precarious and uncertain."[7] Inasmuch as the contemplated railroad would exceed in cost the financial resources of the area, Lincoln still favored the improvement of the Sangamon, a project which he believed completely practicable for vessels of twenty-five to thirty tons. That the river would require extensive improvements was clear. To shorten and straighten the meandering final thirty miles, he suggested the cutting of a direct channel across the low, water-soaked prairie that separated the designated point on the Sangamon from Beardstown, permitting the damned-up river itself to complete the task of preparing the new river channel.

Much of Lincoln's activities in and out of the legislature during the middle and late thirties consisted of road development in central Illinois.[8] He devoted much time to the locating and relocating of roads which connected the major villages of Sangamon County. He introduced bills to build improved roads from Springfield to towns in neighboring counties.[9] In part to achieve his earlier goal of improving the Sangamon River, Lincoln supported a bill in December, 1835, to incorporate the Beardstown and Sangamon Canal Company.[10] Early in January, 1836, he introduced a measure to provide Springfield with state roads to Pekin and Peoria. A year later he added another bill to establish a state road from Springfield to Bloomington. During July, 1837, Lincoln again served the burgeoning interests of Sangamon commerce by introducing a bill to connect Beardstown and the new village of Petersburg, near New Salem, with a state road.[11] At the same time he arranged for the construction of a road from New Salem to Petersburg. Petersburg, with its better location, drew many settlers from New Salem. Indeed, New Salem could not survive its geographical disadvantages and soon became a ghost town.[12]

As a member of the Illinois legislature Lincoln openly favored Clay's national program of public works at federal expense. Running for reelection in June, 1836, he expressed his Whig views unqualifiedly in an open letter to his constituents. "Whether elected or not," he declared, "I go for distributing the proceeds of the sales of the public lands to the several States, to enable our State, in common with others, to dig canals and construct railroads without borrowing money and paying interest on it."[13] Lincoln entered the 1836–37 session of the legislature as head of a project to move the state capital from Vandalia to Springfield, a legislative maneuver which he conducted with perfect success. But the issue that rang through the legislative halls that year was internal improvements, an issue now enlivened by the great financial and population boom of the mid-thirties. Illinois caught an avalanche of settlers who filled much of the wooded regions along the Illinois and Mississippi rivers. When Lincoln moved his residence from New Salem to Springfield in April, 1837, that city had become a busy metropolis. He warned Mary Owens in May that a life of poverty would be decidedly unsatisfactory in a community with so many carriages flourishing about, giving evidence of wealth no less than an established social structure. The transfer of the state capital to Springfield that year enhanced the prestige of the city, brought to it an additional wealth, and reinforced its social cleavage.

Immigrants from Kentucky and Tennessee still avoided the prairies, but new settlers from the East moved by the thousands over and around the Great Lakes into the rich prairies of northern Illinois. Much of that year's hazardous speculation gripped these newly settled prairie regions. "It commenced," wrote Governor Thomas Ford in his *History of Illinois*, "at Chicago, and was the means of building up that place in a year or two from a village of a few houses to be a city of several thousand inhabitants. The story of the sudden fortunes made there excited at first wonder and amazement; next, a gambling spirit of adventure; and lastly, an all-absorbing desire for sudden and splendid wealth."[14] Easterners caught the mania; vessel after vessel unloaded them at the Chicago wharves where they immediately entered the speculation. Towns and cities were laid out in such profusion that some predicted humorously that no land would be left in Illinois for farming.

Still the movement was uneven, leaving unoccupied large areas of rich prairie land in the north central and eastern portions of the state. Clearly Illinois would never achieve an even distribution of population, and thereby reach its full economic potential, without canals and railroads. As early as 1835 the state granted a number of railroad charters, but the stock remained unsold. Meanwhile state leaders proposed a number of railroad surveys to cross the state in various directions, as well as a canal project to connect the Illinois River with Lake Michigan. Indeed, the special session of 1835 authorized a loan of a half million dollars to begin the construction of such a canal. Throughout the summer of 1836 the demand for internal improvements, with the possibilities they offered for speculative profit, was loud and unending. Many candidates far outdid Lincoln in promoting grandiose schemes of railroad building. Late in 1836 an internal improvements convention in Vandalia recommended a statewide rail system supported by a large public loan. Whether a majority of the legislature supported the measure Lincoln would not predict.[15]

Actually the legislature was so fully committed to some program that it quickly devised a network of railroads to serve the underpopulated areas of the state. One projected line would traverse the state from Galena to the mouth of the Ohio; three others would connect Alton on the Mississippi with Shawneetown, Mount Carmel, and the Indiana border via Shelbyville—enough, it seemed, to assure Alton's primacy over St. Louis as a river port. One east-west line, the Northern Cross, would connect Quincy on the Mississippi with the Wabash River in Indiana; shorter lines would join Bloomington with Pekin, and Peoria with Warsaw. Together this proposed rail system would total 1350 miles.[16] Several of the terminal cities were still nonexistent, a measure of the speculative nature of the entire railroad venture. The scheme provided improvements for every stream that could float a shingle. Those areas which could not benefit from these improvements at all would receive a bonus of $200,000 in exchange for their support.

To achieve its objectives the legislature voted $8 million to be raised by a loan. It added $4 million to complete the Illinois-Michigan Canal. The law directed that the work begin simultaneously at the termini of all railroads and at the river crossings. In the continuing speculative frenzy few noticed that the project far exceeded the limits of the state's resources. Lincoln, according to biographers John G. Nicolay and John Hay, voted for the measures and detected no apparent danger in them. He had long favored the improvement of rivers and roads, and as a devoted Whig was content to support the state's upward progress with canals and railroads. But he played no prominent role in the passage of the internal improvement bills, for nothing compelled him to do so.[17]

By the summer of 1837 the Illinois internal improvements program was in serious difficulty. Banks throughout the United States had suspended specie payments. Inasmuch as the hard-pressed state banks of Illinois were the fiscal agents of the railroads and canals, the governor asked the legislature to revise its program and bring it within reasonable bounds. But the mammoth internal improvements scheme had been so extensively oversold that legislators had no choice but to sustain their folly. With borrowed money they ordered construction on a gigantic scale, assuming that the increases in land values along the new routes of commerce would more than compensate for the cost. By 1838 the end was near. Candidates that year were far more reserved. Illinois bonds now glutted the market; the system had failed. The legislature terminated the work. What remained was a huge debt, several miles of embankments, and a few abutments which would wait many years for bridges and trains to cross them.[18]

Lincoln maintained his devotion to the system and accepted its demise with deep regret.[19] In part to resurrect it he proposed in January, 1839, that the state of Illinois purchase from the federal government all unsold public lands lying within the state to give the state both control of all its territory and a new source of revenue. Illinois, argued Lincoln, was

so far advanced in a general system of internal improvements that . . . [it] could not retreat from it, without disgrace and great loss. The conclusion then is, that we *must* advance; and if so, the first reason for the State acquiring title to the public lands is, that while we are at great expense in improving the country, and thereby enhancing the value of all the real property within its limits, that enhancement may attach exclusively to property owned by *ourselves* as a State, or to its citizens as individuals, and *not* to that owned by the Government of the United States. Again, it is conceded every where . . . that Illinois surpasses every other spot of equal extent upon the face of the globe, in *fertility* of soil . . . and consequently that she is endowed by nature with the capacity of sustaining a greater amount of agricultural wealth and population than any other equal extent of territory in the world. To such an amount of wealth and population, our internal improvement system, now so alarming, in view of its having to be borne by our present numbers, and with our present means, would be a burden of no sort of consequence. How important, then, is it that all our energies should be exerted to bring that wealth and population among us as speedily as possible.[20]

Lincoln's proposal had no chance. In January, 1840, Lincoln complained to friends that the "Internal Improvement System will be put down in a lump, without benefit of clergy."[21] That year he advanced measures to sustain the construction of the Illinois-Michigan Canal. To stop work on the canal, he reminded the legislature, would be "much like stopping a skift in the middle of a river—if it was not going up, it *would* go down." [22] Shortly thereafter Lincoln offered an amendment to a bill authorizing the state to issue bonds at par to pay for all subsequent work done on the Illinois-Michigan Canal. He defended the bill by insisting that the state was not prostrated by debt. [23]

With the collapse of the Illinois internal improvement system Lincoln turned his attention to the completion of a single line of railroad from Springfield to the Mississippi at Alton. To achieve that purpose he proposed the Springfield and Alton Turnpike Company in February, 1841, a new company designed to take over and complete the work on that portion of the Alton and Mount Carmel which extended from Alton to its juncture with the Alton and Shelbyville Railroad, then to continue work on the latter line to its intersection with the Central Railroad, to continue northward along the Central until it reached the Northern Cross in Sangamon County. The Springfield and Alton Turnpike Company would be authorized to use as much of the Northern Cross between Jacksonville and Springfield as would serve the interests of the state. When one representative objected that the measure favored one section of the state more than another, Lincoln retorted that "the State property would all be lost and go to ruin, if the principle be adopted that no one shall have any, for fear all shall not have some." [24]

Not until 1846 did the Illinois legislature incorporate the Alton and Springfield railroad to pass from Alton through Carlinville to Springfield, a distance of eighty miles. Lincoln reminded the people of Sangamon County, in an open letter dated June 30, 1847, that construction of the road would rely heavily on eastern capitalists, but he suggested that the people who would benefit directly from the road would encourage the purchase of stock elsewhere simply by buying their share. Adequate returns to pay a substantial interest on the outstanding debt depended obviously on the amount of business which the road carried. For Lincoln the possible impact of the Alton and Springfield on the development of the country through which it passed was almost without limit:

Increase of business would naturally follow, the building of a good road in any country; and this applies especially to this road, by the facts that the country of its line is unequalled in natural agricultural resources, is new, and only yet very partially brought into cultivation. Not one tenth of the land fitted for the plough has yet been subjected to it. Add the *new* fact, that the use of Indian corn has, at length, been successfully introduced into Europe, under circumstances that warrant the hope of its continuance, and the amount of means of transportation which the people of this country must need, is beyond calculation.

Again: at no distant day, a railroad, connecting the Eastern cities with some point on the Mississippi, will surely be built. If we lie by till this be done, it may pass us in such a way as to do us harm rather than good; while, if we complete, or even begin, our road first, it will attract the other, and so become, not merely a local improvement, but a link in one of a great national character, retaining all its local benefits, and superadding many from its general connection.

In view of the foregoing considerations, briefly stated, is it not the interest of us all to *act*, and to act *now*; in this matter? [25]

Clearly the railroad from Alton to Springfield was only one link in a great chain of rail communications which eventually would unite Boston and New York with the Mississippi; it was that prospect alone which made the Alton and Springfield stock attractive to Eastern investors. What endangered the road's completion, however, was the conflicting interest of competing lines which required access to the same track. The original Northern Cross line commenced at Quincy, crossed the Illinois at Meredosia, and extended eastward through Springfield to the Indiana border. Already the state had completed the fifty-seven miles of line from Meredosia to Springfield and had authorized the Alton and Springfield to use the fifteen miles of the completed road from Springfield to New Berlin. Unfortunately, complained the Alton and Springfield committee, the Sangamon and Morgan Railroad Company, incorporated in 1845, owned the line from Meredosia to Springfield and had sole right to extend it from Springfield to the Indiana border. This conflict in ownership and construction rights, the committee feared, could interfere with the completion of the line to Indiana and thereby discourage the needed Eastern investment. The committee argued that the entire line should come under the control of one company and thus eliminate the difficulty arising from conflicting ownership and interests. [26]

Lincoln entered the United States House of Representatives in 1847. There he used the occasion of President James K. Polk's veto of a general internal improvements bill in the spring of 1848 to launch a major defense of Whig doctrine. In his long attack on Polk's veto message and its constitutional philosophy, Lincoln admitted that some districts would benefit more from the federal expenditures than would others. But nothing, he argued, "is so *local* as to not be of some *general* benefit." Improvements on the Mississippi, he reminded the House, would benefit thirteen states. Perhaps the other seventeen would have less interest. Still, he insisted, such improvements would ultimately benefit all. "Take, for instance, the Illinois and Michigan canal," he said. "Considered apart from it's effects, it is perfectly local. Every inch of it is within the state of Illinois. That canal was first opened for business last April. In a very few days we were all gratified to learn, among other things, that sugar had been carried from New Orleans through this canal to Buffalo in New York." [27]

Denying the Democratic dogma that internal improvements were unconstitutional, Lincoln averred that at issue was not the Constitution, but expediency, and for matters of expediency he had a ready answer. "The true rule, in determining to embrace, or reject any thing," he said, "is not whether it have *any* evil in it; but whether it have more of evil, than of good. There are few things *wholly* evil, or *wholly* good. Almost every thing, especially of governmental policy, is an inseparable compound of the two; so that our best judgment of the preponderance between them is continually demanded." [28] Lincoln again explained the relationship he detected between internal improvements and economic progress:

Such products of the country as are to be *consumed* where they are *produced*, need no roads or rivers—no means of transportation, and have no very proper connection with this subject. The *surplus*—that which is produced in *one* place, to be consumed in *another*; the capacity of each locality for producing a *greater* surplus; the natural means of transportation, and their susceptability of improvement; the hindrances, delays, and losses of life and property during transportation, and the causes of each, would be among the most valuable statistics. . . . From these, it would readily appear where a given amount of expenditure would do the most good. These statistics might be equally accessible, as they would be equally useful, to both the nation and the states. In this way, and by these means, let the nation take hold of the larger works, and the states the smaller ones; and thus, working in a meeting direction, discreetly, but steadily and firmly, what is made unequal in one place may be equalized in another, extravagance avoided, and the whole country put on that career of prosperity, which shall correspond with it's extent of teritory, it's natural resources, and the intelligence and enterprize of it's people.[29]

Lincoln's interest in railroad development continued into the fifties. During 1851 the newly formed Alton and Sangamon Railroad Company retained him in several suits to compel stockholders to pay past-due installments on their shares of stock. The "Alton" railroad reached Springfield in September, 1852. Already the extension to Chicago was under construction. Lincoln, meanwhile, was an incorporator of the Springfield and Terre Haute Railroad. Since the forties the Illinois legislature had obstructed every transportation system which might contribute directly to the prosperity of any major city outside Illinois. In keeping with that principle, Lincoln opposed the establishment of the Atlantic and Mississippi Railroad in 1854, for this line, projected to terminate at Illinoistown, opposite St. Louis, and not at Alton, would bring greater benefits to Missouri than to Illinois.[30]

During the period from 1853 to 1860 Lincoln handled numerous cases for the Illinois Central Railroad in the Eighth Judicial District in central Illinois, no fewer than eleven cases before the Illinois Supreme Court, and at least one case before the federal court in Chicago. Indeed, during the 1850s the Illinois Central became Lincoln's major client. Fees for small cases dealing with trespass, right-of-way, property damage, injury to livestock, or freight claims were exceedingly modest. On September 14, 1855, Lincoln wrote to Illinois Central General Counsel James F. Joy of Chicago: "I have to day drawn on you in favor of the McLean County Bank, or rather it's cashier, for one hundred and fifty dollars. This is intended as a fee for all services done by me for the Illinois Central Railroad, since last September, within the counties of McLean and DeWitt. Within that term, and in the two counties, I have assisted, for the Road, in at least fifteen cases . . . and I have concluded to lump them off at ten dollars a case. With this explanation, I shall be obliged if you will honor the draft."[31] In his most celebrated Illinois Central case Lincoln defended the road against McLean County's attempt to levy a property tax against it. For Lincoln this was a case of major significance. He lost the case in the local court in 1853, but argued it before the Illinois Supreme Court in February, 1854, and again in January, 1856.

This time he won the case and collected the unusual fee of five thousand dollars for his successful effort.

Lincoln's most famous defense of Western railroad interests came in *Hurd v. Rock Island Bridge Company* (1857). The Rock Island railroad bridge, the first across the Mississippi, became the center of a struggle between the railroad and steamboat interests when, in May, 1856, shortly after its completion, the steamboat *Effie Afton* crashed into one of the bridge's piers and burned. In the process it destroyed a span of the bridge. The *Afton* owners brought suit against the bridge company and immediately received backing from the steamboat interests along the river as well as from the St. Louis Chamber of Commerce which accurately viewed the controversy as a contest between St. Louis and Chicago for the commerce of the Upper Mississippi Valley.[32] The trial was held at the federal court in Chicago, September 8–24, 1857. Lincoln's widely-reported defense came on September 22 and 23. He began by recognizing the interest of St. Louis in the case, for the removal of the bridge would obviously advance its river commerce. He would not, he added, care to see a great channel that extended from where it never freezes to where it never thaws blocked up. But there was also, he said, an East-West trade of equal if not greater importance to the nation, building up new regions with a rapidity never before seen in the history of the world. Whereas the Mississippi was closed to transportation almost four months in 1856, the bridge was open every day of its existence. Such a structure, said Lincoln, merited the respect of the court.

As a legally built structure, Lincoln continued, a bridge could demand greater skill and care of the pilots who passed under it. Lincoln answered the plaintiffs' charge that the piers changed the direction and speed of the current sufficiently to make the passage dangerous by insisting that the *Afton* had sufficient speed upstream to pass under the bridge without difficulty. But the *Afton*, Lincoln charged, had passed another boat that was on true course and thus approached the bridge across the current, compelling the pilot to lose control. A tunnel under the river, said Lincoln, was not feasible; a suspension bridge could never rise so high that the chimneys of the boats could not reach it. Lincoln concluded: "The plaintiffs have to establish that the bridge is a material obstruction, and that they managed their boat with reasonable care and skill. As to the last point, high winds have nothing to do with it, for it was not a windy day. They must show 'due skill and care.' Difficulties going down stream, will not do, for they were going up stream. Difficulties with barges in tow, have nothing to do with it, for they had no barge." [33] The Chicago jury, splitting nine for the bridge and three against, failed to arrive at a verdict. The litigation continued until 1862 when the United States Supreme Court decided in favor of the bridge company.

By 1860 the Illinois railroad system had achieved its basic outline. The road from Alton to Springfield reached Bloomington in October, 1853; one year later it reached Chicago. The east-west railroad through Springfield now extended from Quincy to Danville and the Indiana border where it connected with lines to Indianapolis and the major cities of Ohio and the Atlantic coast. To the south two important lines connected Alton and St. Louis with important Indiana towns. Routes from Chicago reached the Mississippi at Galena, Clinton, Davenport, Burlington, Quincy, Alton, and Cairo. Illinois experienced its major population growth of the fifties where the railroads crossed the great open prairies. "In 1853," wrote John W. Foster, geologist of the Illinois Central, "I traversed the route [Of the Illinois Central] between Chicago and Urbana, a distance of more than 125 miles. It passed through a nearly unbroken prairie, with here and there a house by the margin of a wooded belt. Now [1856] the traveler never loses sight of cultivated farms, and at intervals of at least every ten miles are flourishing villages with all the appliances of civilized life." [34] Areas such as the Sangamon country, with their record of earlier settlement, developed more slowly. Still no region of the state had been totally untouched by the completion of the state's railway network.

For Lincoln the development of improved transportation in Illinois from roads to railroads had been, through three fateful decades, a matter of major concern. He was first among those who refused to desert the massive internal improvements system of 1836 after its collapse. Thereafter he supported each new project with enthusiasm. Lincoln could boast in February, 1859, that the United States, with its greater experimentation, had outstripped the rest of the world in the application of steam and water power to industry and transportation. Even then the great challenge to American ingenuity was the development of the nation's resources, and the opportunities thus created for public convenience and private gain provided ample compensation for the effort. Lincoln could assume that the nation's resources were without limit and that the wealth created by their use would serve the best interests of society. He could scarcely foresee the time, a century later, when the space and resources which appeared so limitless would begin to vanish; nor could he anticipate the waste, pollution, and environmental disaster which would ultimately exceed what even a rich country could afford. But if Lincoln no less than his contemporaries measured progress in terms of increased productivity, speed, and comfort, he favored decent procedures in the application of capital and technology to economic processes to assure both a maximum of efficiency and a minimum of waste.

Lincoln's notions of progress encompassed all aspects of economic and social advancement, individual as well as national. He assumed that men who were industrious, sober, and honest would, in the pursuit of their own interests, accumulate capital and thereafter possess the means to employ others to work for them. "The hired laborer of yesterday," wrote Lincoln, "labors on his own account to-day; and will hire others to labor for him to-morrow. Advancement—improvement in condition—is the order of things in a society of equals."[35] This relationship between capital and labor was not only a proper one but also one that would bring a maximum of individual and social progress. For free labor had the inspiration of hope, and the power of hope upon human exertion and happiness, believed Lincoln, was limitless.

What mattered in agricultural progress was the exchange of agricultural discovery, information, and knowledge "so that, at the end, *all* may know every thing, which may have been known to but *one*, or to but a *few*, at the beginning."[36] Lincoln favored not only the application of invention to agricultural production but also greater thoroughness in cultivation, preferring that farmers maximize production per acre rather than extend their cultivation to larger acreages, usually at the price of more slovenly practices. For to him the major gains in production would come from the quality of the effort. not the number of acres cultivated. "Population must increase rapidly—more rapidly than in former times," he reminded a Milwaukee audience in September, 1859, "and ere long the most valuable of all arts, will be the art of deriving a comfortable subsistence from the smallest area of soil. No community whose every member possesses this art, can ever be the victim of oppression in any of its forms."[37]

Lincoln assumed, finally, that individual Americans would best improve their condition through education. "The thought recurs," he said, "that education—cultivated thought—can best be combined with agricultural labor, or any labor, on the principle of thorough work—that careless, half performed, slovenly work, makes no place for such combination." It was ultimately the quality of life and performance that created a civilization of progress and excellence. Lincoln accepted the validity of the old admonition, "And this, too, shall pass away." Yet, he added, "let us hope it is not quite true. Let us hope, rather, that by the best cultivation of the physical world, beneath and around us; and the intellectual and moral world within us, we shall secure an individual, social, and political prosperity and happiness, whose course shall be onward and upward, and which, while the earth endures, shall not pass away."[38] If Lincoln's major political and intellectual efforts after 1854 dwelt largely on the issue of slavery and its extension, he remained ever conscious of the country's progress and the contribution of individual effort, invention, education, and improved transportation to that progress.

With the country trapped in a deepening sectional crisis, Lincoln, in early 1861, readied his departure for Washington. Standing before his friends and well-wishers at Springfield's railroad depot on February 11, he recalled the meaning of his long residence in Sangamon County.

No one [he said], not in my situation, can appreciate my feeling of sadness at this parting. To this place, and the kindness of these people, I owe every thing. Here I have lived a quarter of a century, and have passed from a young to an old man. Here my children have been born, and one is buried. I now leave, not knowing when, or whether ever, I may return, with a task before me greater than that which rested upon Washington. Without the assistance of that Divine Being, who ever attended him, I cannot succeed. With that assistance I cannot fail. Trusting in Him, who can go with me, and remain with you and be every where for good, let us confidently hope that all will yet be well. To His care commending you, as I hope in your prayers you will commend me, I bid you an affectionate farewell.[39]

Lincoln's train moved eastward, passed through Tolono and Danville, crossed the Indiana line, and six hours later slowed to a halt at Lafayette.

SIX

The Search for Order and Community

GEORGE M. FREDRICKSON

Recent scholarship has viewed Abraham Lincoln from almost every conceivable vantage point except that of American intellectual history. There have of course been studies of Lincoln's thought: Harry V. Jaffa has written incisively on his political philosophy, William J. Wolf has analyzed his religious beliefs, and Edmund Wilson has brilliantly assessed his contribution to the literature of the Civil War.[1] But none of these writers have been primarily concerned with locating Lincoln's ideas in some larger pattern of social and cultural thought. What they have shown is that Lincoln had an active intellect, a powerful imagination, and a strong desire to expose the fundamental principles underlying the political controversies in which he was engaged. But to appreciate fully Lincoln's contribution to the growth of American thought, we have to know more about his basic intellectual style—where it came from, what its essential characteristics were, how it related to other modes of thought, and how it influenced Lincoln's response to the events of the time.

Before the slavery issue swallowed up or absorbed all other concerns in the 1850s, a major preoccupation of the American mind was determining the proper limits, if any, for a militant and aggressive democracy, usually associated with the extension of the suffrage, the rise of Jacksonianism, and a corresponding decline of popular deference to the established political and social elites of the revolutionary and federal periods. Thoughtful Americans differed markedly in how they responded to these developments. There was of course a "party of hope," which celebrated democritization in all its forms and manifestations. Believing that the voice of the people was indeed the voice of God, radical democrats repudiated the leadership of a cultivated class that stood for both the claims of the intellect and the vested rights of property and hailed instead the untutored feelings and intuitions of the common man as the proper foundation for government and community. In terms of the head-heart dichotomy so central to the nineteenth-century imagination, they stood for a democracy of the heart. In so doing, they broke with some of their own patron saints and with the Enlightenment conception of American republicanism. According to John William Ward, the shift from Jeffersonian to Jacksonian democracy constituted, among other things, a retreat from the view that reason or disciplined intelligence was the mainstay of popular government. The new faith put its trust in "the prompting of man's heart" or, in more metaphysical terms, in the access of every man to a "higher reason of nature" deemed vastly superior to the more calculating reason of academicians, lawyers, and highly educated men generally.[2]

From the 1820s to the 1850s romantic democracy was the popular creed of the American people. It manifested itself in the cult of Jackson as "Nature's Nobleman"—a rough-hewn genius emerging from the wilderness, whose native instincts gave him an intuitive grasp of the popular will denied to those who had spent too much time in their drawing rooms or studies.[3] It was reflected too in a characteristic impatience with laws, charters, and established procedures that could be seen as restraints on the direct expression of majority opinion. Jackson's own cavalier disregard of legal technicalities in the bank struggle and of Supreme Court decisions involving Indian rights contributed to the growing contempt for the letter of the law and the authority of courts or other institutions that claimed immunity from the immediate demands of the populace or its spokesmen.[4]

As David Grimsted has pointed out, this "refusal to accept the sanctity of the law had its most disruptive manifestation in the long series of riots in the Jacksonian period."[5] The innumerable riots, "tumults," and lynchings which occurred in the 1830s and 1840s had their immediate origin in ethnic or religious animosities, popular hostility to abolitionists, anger at defaulting bankers, or a desire to impose order and decorum on lawless or disreputable elements in frontier communities. But the ultimate sanction for mob violence was an extreme version of "romantic democracy"—a widespread belief that nothing should stand in the way of spontaneous popular feeling. Some Jacksonian theorists even defended mob action in principle. One of them, Francis Grund, contended that lynching was "not properly speaking an opposition to the established laws of the country . . . , but rather . . . a supplement to them—as a species of *common law.*"[6]

Those Americans, usually described as "conservatives," who refused to worship at the shrine of unrestrained popular emotion, may perhaps be forgiven for resisting what seemed to them like a trend toward general anarchy or majority tyranny. If romantic democracy was carried to its logical extreme, aroused local majorities would presumably have had absolute power over the life, liberty, and property of unpopular classes, minorities, and individuals. To prevent this from happening, men with more traditional conceptions of order and community mounted a substantial counterattack against the ideas and practices associated with the radical democratic impulse.

It would be a serious error, however, to see this "conservative" response as monolithic or single-minded. There were in fact two distinct and seemingly contradictory conceptions of how the Republic could be saved from anarchy or mobocracy. One placed its reliance on evangelical religion and found its principal spokesmen in an important segment of the Protestant clergy. The other was associated with the rise of the legal profession and sought to inculcate respect for law and established procedures among the citizenry by demonstrating the rational principles underlying the legal and constitutional order. If the clergy represented a conservatism of the heart in its insistence that Christian piety was the only safe and sure foundation of respect for law and established authority, the lawyers stood for a conservatism of the head and a greater respect for the rationalistic or Enlightenment sources of the American polity.[7]

The evangelical perspective was ably set forth by the *Christian Spectator* in 1829:

"What has religion to do with the State?" you ask. In the form of ecclesiastical alliances, nothing; but in its operation as a controlling, purifying power in the consciences of the people, we answer, it has every thing to do, it is the last hope of republics; and let it be remembered, if ever our ruin shall come, that the questions which agitate, the factions which distract, the convulsions which dissolve, will be secondary causes: The true evil will lie back of these, in the moral debasement of the people; and no excellence of political institutions, no sagacity of human wisdom, which did not, like that of our Puritan fathers, begin and end with religion, could have averted the calamity.[8]

Fifteen years later, in a massive tome entitled *Religion in America*, the Reverend Robert Baird sounded a more hopeful note by celebrating the conservative impact of revivals and organized benevolence. It is, he contended, in "the immense moral influence of the church," as manifested in evangelical preaching, Sunday schools, Bible classes, and other organized Christian activities, "that the laws find their surest basis and most effective sanction."[9]

The logical tendency of the evangelical movement, in the North at least, was toward a kind of informal theocracy—a re-creation of the essence of Puritan New England along voluntaristic lines, with controlled revivals, home missionary work, and moral reform societies performing the disciplinary and stabilizing functions formerly carried out by established churches and pious magistrates. But in their efforts to establish a moral community, the evangelicals ran the risk of arousing the passion for righteousness to such an intensity that it could threaten the social peace by denying the validity of laws and established institutions which conflicted with a perfectionist interpretation of Christian ethics. Hence the revival helped spawn a militant antislavery movement and a growing conviction that human laws deserved respect only if they were ratified by the "higher law" of Christian conscience.[10] Even the more conservative Northern evangelicals tended to see slavery as a major threat to their ideal of national salvation and were prepared to view the aggressive "slave power" of the 1840s and 1850s as combining with a Godless democracy to undermine their campaign for a cohesive social order based on Christian faith and morality.

The legal profession responded to romantic democracy in a much more sober and worldly fashion. The juridical mind of course gave the central role in the maintenance of order and community to practical-minded lawyers and judges rather than to evangelical clergymen (who might turn out to be dangerous fanatics). Rufus Choate, one of the luminaries of the antebellum bar, described the lawyer as the most useful kind of American professional because it was his unique responsibility to "preserve our organic forms, our civil and social order, our constitutions of government,—even the Union itself."[11] Lawyers did not usually deny the salutary effects of organized religion. But, as Perry Miller has brilliantly demonstrated, they sought not only to confine Christianity to an essentially private sphere but also cultivated an intellectual style quite distinct from that of the evangelicals. In an age of romanticism, when conservative revivalists as well as radical spokesmen for secular democracy tended to rely on feeling and intuition as the source of communal attachments, leaders of the bench and the bar stood rock-firm for the reign of cultivated reason, for the dominance of the intellect over the emotions. At a time when "genius," whether in the role of a tribune of a people like Andrew Jackson or a charismatic revivalist like Charles G. Finney, was much revered, the lawyers persisted in emphasizing the neoclassical ideal of the reasonable man.[12]

These predilections were reflected in a distinctive response to the threat to order and stability presented by the trend toward radical democracy. For the legal mind of the antebellum period, the main barriers to mobocracy were the common law tradition and American constitutionalism, both of which they interpreted primarily in terms of restraint. When there had been a king, the function of law was to restrain the royal power in its efforts to interfere with the personal and property rights of subjects. Now that there was no king, the greatest threat to liberty and property came from popular majorities.[13] In the new situation, as in the old, the greatest safety lay in a competent and respected bar, an independent judiciary, and in a popular awareness of the rational principle that a violation of the rights of some threatened the rights of all. The lawyers were thus much closer than the clergymen to the natural law foundations of the American republic, and it was the great paradox of their thought that their conservatism often had a liberal foundation.[14] While the conservative clergy sometimes denigrated the thinking that surrounded the Declaration of Independence as "atheistic"—or, at any rate, insufficiently Christian—because of its failure to acknowledge the divine sanction for "the powers that be," the lawyers tended to adhere to the eighteenth-century view that government was simply a man-made contractual arrangement to protect the natural rights of individuals.

Of course the lawyers, and especially the judges, had their own problems with the relation of natural law to positive law. Most saw their role as the interpretation and application of positive law even when it seemed to conflict with natural justice, as in cases involving slavery. This gave rise to the problems of conscience that Robert Cover has described in his fine study of the judicial response to antislavery. To reconcile the conflict many legalists had recourse to "the doctrine of necessity," the idea that the first priority of any society was survival and that natural law should not be carried to the point where it threatened the maintenance of the social order. Antislavery initiatives which conflicted with law protecting slavery were often viewed in this light, even by judges who acknowledged the fundamental injustice of servitude.[15]

In the last analysis, the legalists placed their faith in procedure, in regular and established ways of making decisions and resolving disputes. For most of them, communities were composed of individuals who were able to live together only because they agreed to submit their varying and sometimes conflicting claims to some form of prescribed and rational adjudication. No higher motive than enlightened self-interest was required to induce compliance to the rules. The great enemy, then, was the kind of "passion" or irrationality that would lead the angry, the greedy, or even the intensely moral or pious, to disregard their real interests in the pursuit of the kind of immediate gratifications that could only be found outside of law and established procedures.

Both the evangelicals with their concept of a moral community and the legalists with their ideal of a procedural community were, as might be expected, predominantly Whig in their political loyalties in the 1830s and 1840s. But there is good reason to doubt whether either could find in the Whig program of internal improvements and protective tariffs an adequate vehicle for their fundamental concerns about the drift toward disorder and chaotic democracy. Some of the extraordinary intensity and success of the Republican party in the North in the 1850s can perhaps be attributed to the way it was able to use the issue of slavery extension to appeal to some of the deepest anxieties of both groups.

Abraham Lincoln's early speeches as an aspiring young lawyer and Whig politician were clearly part of this "conservative" response to the unruly and aggressive democracy spawned by the age of Jackson. His first exposition of the law and order theme was in a speech to the Illinois legislature on January 11, 1837. As a Whig stalwart, Lincoln was opposing a Democratic bill calling for an investigation of the state bank, and he accused the proponents of the measure of demagoguery, of "endeavoring to blow up a storm" for their own political advantage. He opposed the examination of the bank, not only because it proceeded from such questionable motives, but also because he viewed it as beyond the legal authority of the legislature. "I am opposed," he said, "to encouraging that lawless and mobocratic spirit, whether in relation to the bank or any thing else, which is already abroad in the land; and is spreading with rapid and fearful impetuosity, to the ultimate overthrow of every institution, or even moral principle, in which persons and property have hitherto found security." It would be difficult to find a more succinct statement of the basic conservative response to the romantic democracy of the 1830s.[16]

Almost exactly a year later, on January 27, 1838, Lincoln developed the same general theme on a less partisan occasion and in a more systematic and reflective way. In his address before the Young Men's Lyceum of Springfield, he directed his attention not to the allegedly extralegal machinations of the Democratic party but to an even more dramatic manifestations of the "lawless and mobocratic spirit"—the outbreak of riots and lynchings that had recently occurred throughout the country. He began with a eulogy to the nation's founders who had raised "a political edifice of equality and equal rights." The current generation should not try to improve on this achievement; its only duty was to preserve and transmit what the founders had erected. The great present danger to American political institutions, he warned, came from "the increasing disregard for law which pervades the country; the growing disposition to substitute the wild and furious passions, in lieu of the sober judgment of Courts; and the worse than savage mobs, for the executive ministers of justice." [17] Unless such actions ceased, general chaos would result and the "*attachment*" of the people to their government would be destroyed. The only way to "fortify" against this threat was "to instill the reverence for law in every American" until it had become "the *political religion*" of the nation.[18]

In the next section of his speech Lincoln warned about the special problem presented by men of genius. During the revolutionary era those with an intense craving for "celebrity, fame and distinction" had found fulfillment in the great experiment of establishing a self-governing republic. But that work was done, and such men could no longer be expected to find "their ruling passion" gratified by the mundane work of upholding an edifice constructed by others. "Towering genius disdains the beaten path" and will now seek glory and distinction in ways that threaten the established order, "whether at the expense of emancipating slaves, or enslaving freemen." To frustrate the designs of such a man, "it will require the people to be united with each other, attached to the government and laws, and generally intelligent." [19]

Lincoln spoke for his age in identifying "towering genius" with the reign of the emotions over the intellect, and he went on to discourse more generally on the relation of "the *passions*" to the problem of "maintaining our institutions." The Revolution, and for sometime afterward the memory of it, had enlisted all the passions, including the basest, on the side of liberty. But those days were now gone. "Passion has helped us; but can do so no more. It will in future be our enemy. Reason, cold, calculating, unimpassioned reason, must furnish all the materials for our future support and defence." [20]

This remarkable speech has led to some provocative speculations on Lincoln's psychology. Interpreters of Lincoln have been struck by the comments on "genius" and have debated its relevance to his personal ambitions and possible sense of himself as a man of destiny. [21] Actually it was not at all unusual for a lawyer to deprecate genius or defend calculating reason against exalted passion. It was, as we have seen, an integral part of the juridical defense of a procedural community. Lincoln was thus giving eloquent expression to the developing ideology of his profession as it confronted the challenge of romantic democracy, and not making a unique personal statement. [22]

As a proponent of the rational-legalistic or procedural concept of order and community, the young Lincoln could scarcely have been much attracted to the alternative "conservative" philosophy—the ideal of a church-centered, moral community. We know of course that Lincoln never joined a church or belonged to a moral reform society and was in fact something of a freethinker by the strict standards of the time. He did address the Washington Temperance Society in 1842, but only, it seems, to praise their particular kind of self-help reformism (which anticipated the Alcoholics Anonymous of our time) at the expense of the more orthodox and authoritarian crusades directed by the clergy. Preachers were not the best advocates of temperance, Lincoln told the Washingtonians, because they could readily be suspected of fanaticism and of desiring "a union of Church and State." The great failing of the "old school" temperance reformers was their habit of berating drunkards "in the thundering tones of anathema and denunciation," thus alienating those they should have been trying to convert. "If you would win a man to your cause," Lincoln advised, "*first* convince him that you are his sincere friend.

Therein is a drop of honey that catches his heart, which, say what he will, is the great high road to his reason, and which, when once gained, you will find but little trouble in convincing his judgment of the justice of your cause, if indeed that cause be really a just one."[23]

Lincoln of course had to tread carefully. It was risky for a politician, especially a Whig politician, to attack the clergy and its campaigns for moral reform too openly. But it seems clear that the temperance speech was in part a veiled criticism of the emotionalism and self-righteousness of the theocratic reformers, including those who were tending toward a denunciatory abolitionism; it was in fact an implicit denial of their whole concept of a community based on moral exhortation and intimidation.

This rationalistic concern for order remained a central component of Lincoln's more mature thought and strongly influenced his response to the deepening sectional conflict of the 1850s. His famous attacks on the Kansas-Nebraska Act and the principle of popular sovereignty were often similar in spirit to his earlier reactions to "lawless" democracy or "mobocracy." In his speeches from 1854 to 1860, Lincoln attacked the notion that slavery in the territories could be "voted up or down" by local majorities as a violation of the natural law foundations of American government that could in no way be justified by "the doctrine of necessity." Furthermore, it repudiated what he regarded as the precedent of slavery limitation set by the founding fathers and embodied in the Missouri Compromise. In short, it was a new and even more dangerous manifestation of the "mobocratic" tendency—a logical extension of the kind of amoral and extralegal democracy that condoned lynching or the right of legislative bodies to ride roughshod over binding precedents and established procedures. The adamant stand of the Republicans against the expansion of slavery, on the other hand, was for him the only position fully consistent with an enlightened and conscientious conservatism. In a speech at Columbus, Ohio, on September 16, 1859, Lincoln described the "chief and real purpose of the Republican Party" as "eminently conservative," because it sought "nothing save and except to restore this government to its original tone in regard to this element of slavery, and there to maintain it, looking for no further change, in reference to it, than that which the original framers of the government themselves expected and looked forward to."[24] His argument that the Republicans advocated no new principles or policies but simply a reasonable application of established precedent was most fully developed in the main body of his famous Cooper Union speech of February 27, 1860.[25]

Characteristically, then, Lincoln argued for the maintenance of "free soil" in terms that were compatible with the rational-legalistic tradition. When he spoke directly of slaveholding Southerners, he generally called for a tolerant understanding of their predicament and a firm acknowledgment of their rights under the Constitution to be free of federal interference with slavery where it already existed and to have their fugitive slaves returned. His position as a moderate Republican set him off from the radicals and abolitionists, who tended to speak in the tones of moral absolutism and higher law deriving from the evangelical tradition and to denounce the "slave power" as sinful rather than merely unfortunate and misguided. Where Lincoln generally appealed to reason, the more radical Free-Soilers and abolitionists sought to arouse feelings of moral righteousness and create the atmosphere of a religious crusade.

When Lincoln confronted the secession crisis as president-elect, he presented himself primarily as defender of law and order, a champion of the procedural community against those who refused to abide by a public decision constitutionally arrived at. If the demands of the South that the Republicans repudiate their principles were "acquiesced in," he warned, they "would not merely be the ruin of a man, or a party; but as a precedent they would ruin the government itself."[26] As Philip S. Paludan has suggested, Lincoln was probably speaking for a Northern majority in seeing the Civil War itself as "a crisis in law and order," or, in our terms, as a challenge to the ideal of a procedural community which the legal profession had helped to inculcate in the public mind. If the South were allowed to secede, the whole structure of orderly self-government would be undermined, because the precedent would be set for any group which disagreed with the law of the land, or with a public decision arrived at through regular and constitutional procedures, to take matters into its own hands.[27]

To leave it at that, however, would be to pigeonhole Lincoln too neatly and to ignore the element of change and dialectical complexity in his later thought. The Lincoln of the 1850s was not purely and simply what he had been in the late 1830s—a conservative of the rational-legalistic persuasion. As he wrestled with the slavery issue after 1854 his own feelings and moral passions tended to be aroused. In his famous letter to his old friend Joshua Speed in 1855, Lincoln confessed his personal revulsion to slavery and asked the proslavery Speed, now residing in Kentucky, "to appreciate how much the great body of the Northern people do crucify their feelings, in order to maintain their loyalty to the constitution and the Union."[28] Although he tried for a time to repress these feelings, they came into the open in 1858 when the nature of the senatorial contest with Douglas forced him to rest his case on the proposition that slavery was morally wrong.[29] By the time of the Cooper Union speech Lincoln was operating on two distinct levels. The bulk of the address was in the restrained tradition of rational-legal persuasion, but it ended with a thunderous exhortation to men with antislavery convictions: "Neither let us be slandered from our duty by false accusations against us, nor frightened from it by menaces of destruction to the Government nor of dungeons to ourselves. LET US HAVE FAITH THAT RIGHT MAKES MIGHT, AND IN THAT FAITH, LET US TO THE END, DARE TO DO OUR DUTY AS WE UNDERSTAND IT."[30] Although he continued to be strongly influenced by the juridical style and ideology, Lincoln was clearly making some concessions to the spirit of evangelical antislavery by acknowledging a profound moral dimension in the struggle that presumably transcended purely legal and procedural considerations. If most of the Cooper Union speech was directed at the sober judgment of a jury of reasonable men, the conclusion appealed to the emotions of a community that had been morally aroused by the antislavery crusade.

Furthermore, there is an aspect of Lincoln's response to secession which suggests a different kind of movement beyond the strict confines of conservative legalism. Besides denouncing secession as unconstitutional and a threat to law and order, he also made the surprisingly radical suggestion that the ultimate authority for interpreting the Constitution was a majority of the people. In his speech at Steubenville, Ohio, on February 14, 1861, Lincoln argued that the controversy over the rights of the South under the Constitution could properly be decided only by "the voice of the people." For, "If the majority does not control, the minority must—would that be right?"[31] Here, and in his call in the first inaugural for "a patient confidence in the ultimate justice of the people," Lincoln was implying that the popular will, rather than an elite of lawyers and judges, should be entrusted to interpret the constitutional foundations of American government.[32] It was probably the *Dred Scot* decision, more than anything else, that had shaken Lincoln's faith in the bench and bar as the ultimate arbiters of constitutional issues. In any case, his claim for the sovereignty of a national majority, even over the Constitution itself, represented a break with the elitist implications of the juridical ideology and an accommodation to the spirit, if not to the methods, of Jacksonian democracy.

Lincoln's tendency in the period from 1854 to 1861 to absorb and adapt conflicting conceptions of the sources of order and community in America foreshadowed his great intellectual achievement—the new synthesis of American ideals that he achieved in his eloquent speeches of the war years. In these addresses, especially the Gettysburg Address and the second inaugural, he in effect transcended the antebellum disputes by interpreting the meaning of the war in a way that brought together legalistic concepts of order, the ideal of majoritarian democracy, and a religious sense of American destiny.

His essential proposition that the war for the Union was also a struggle for the democratic principle, a test of whether "government of the people, by the people, and for the people" could endure, can be seen as a successful effort to place the democratic ethos within a new framework of national order and purpose. His acknowledgment in the second inaugural that the nation's suffering was a judgment of God for the "offense" of slaveholding echoed the evangelical Christian view that a people that had forgotten God in its zeal for the wealth produced by slaves deserved divine retribution; yet in Lincoln's formulation the providential interpretation of history was accompanied by a recognition that the guilt was shared by both North and South. Hence he could call for a spirit of forgiveness and moderation rather than accepting the characteristic evangelical view that the war was a holy crusade—an Armageddon between the children of light and the children of darkness.

In his pronouncements on the meaning of the war, therefore, Lincoln can be seen as striving to lay the foundations for a new conception of order and community in America which synthesized the compatible elements of the three points of view that had struggled for dominion in the antebellum period. He conceived of the embattled North as a popular democracy in which the people could be trusted; indeed its central commitment to law, order, and stability was being demonstrated in the most conclusive way possible—on the battlefield and through the sacrifice of blood and treasure. Furthermore the struggle was in accordance with some divine purpose and could legitimately arouse religious emotions. Such a synthesis of the spirit of democracy, the sanctity of the laws, and the sense of religious mission constituted a striking fulfillment of the search for a viable sense of national purpose that had been the great intellectual drama of the antebellum period. Unfortunately, it also laid the foundation for a new American self-righteousness that would have destructive consequences when the nation embarked upon its later career of imperial expansion and international confrontation. But Lincoln can hardly be blamed for this. His own vision was a purely domestic one; his expectation of America's international role as "the last, best hope of earth," was, like Jefferson's, based on the power of example and not the example of power.

If Lincoln was no protoimperialist, he was even less a forerunner of those modern conservatives who call for a rigid and emotional adherence to traditional modes of thought and behavior. His mature attitude toward essential change was stated with great eloquence in his annual message to Congress on December 1, 1862: "The dogmas of the quiet past, are inadequate to the stormy present. The occasion is piled high with difficulty, and we must rise with the occasion. As our case is new, so we must think anew. . . . We must disenthrall ourselves, and then we shall save our country."[33]

The lesson for the present in Lincoln's thought stems less from the specifics of his nineteenth-century ideology than from this general recognition that preservation of the kind of order and stability essential to any good society may sometimes require radical innovation. Furthermore, we can learn much from his conviction that short-sighted efforts to maintain social harmony by ignoring fundamental conflicts of principle actually promote the kind of chaos they are designed to prevent. The idea that an enlightened conservatism can be the inspiration for reform or even revolution is alien to the simplistic right-left or conservative-liberal dichotomy of contemporary political language. In our own troubled times, we need to recapture Lincoln's essential insight that the spirit of innovation and the search for order are not incompatible but are inseparable aspects of a single process—the never-ending quest for a responsible politics and a just society.

PART 3

Lincoln, Politics, and War

SEVEN

Lincoln, Douglas, and Springfield in the 1858 Campaign

CHRISTOPHER N. BREISETH

Springfield, Illinois, in 1858 was of strategic importance to the political fortunes of Stephen A. Douglas, perhaps the most important political figure in the country, and to Abraham Lincoln, who in two years would become the most important political figure. The central Illinois political base for Douglas and Lincoln, Springfield and Sangamon County reflected and affected the issues shaping the careers of these longtime rivals as they fought for a seat in the United States Senate.

Springfield was something of a prairie Philadelphia in 1858. In and around the statehouse and the courthouse political activity was at a fever pitch. Throughout the year, statewide and county conventions and party caucuses for the Douglas Democrats, the Buchanan Democrats, the Fillmore Americans, and the Republicans met in Springfield to fashion the platforms and strategies each carried into the campaign of summer and fall. Representatives from all parts of Illinois, from Chicago to Cairo, from Galena and Quincy to Danville and Charleston, converged repeatedly on this capital city, estimated by contemporaries to include thirteen thousand, to debate issues threatening to tear the country apart.[1] Illinois, because of its geographical position between North and South, East and West, its economic diversity, and its population coming from both the North and South, as well as from Europe, contained nearly all the major perspectives contending that year throughout the country. From abolitionists to advocates of slavery, with perhaps the largest proportion wanting to compromise the differences, the men of Illinois seemed to understand that they were grappling with the nation's survival. They repeatedly referred to the founders of the Constitution and redebated the meaning and appropriateness of the Declaration of Independence, particularly the phrase "that all men are created equal." More than political advantage was involved in this ritual. These sons of the Northwest, conscious of the novelty of self-government, were determined to maintain and nurture in the face of threats of disunion the grand experiment begun by their forefathers eighty-two years earlier.

All parties agreed that central Illinois held the key to the November election when voters would elect a legislature which in turn would select the United States senator. Northern Illinois, with strong antislavery sentiment, was conceded to the Republicans while southern Illinois was judged safe for the Douglas Democracy. If Illinois represented a cross section of the nation, central Illinois including Sangamon County reflected a cross section of the state. Persuading this constituency was crucial for both sides. From the strategically located capital city, the *Illinois State Register* sounded the call for Stephen A. Douglas and the *Illinois State Journal* put out the word for Abraham Lincoln. Charles H. Lanphier and Edward Conner, editors of the *Register*, and Edward L. Baker and William H. Bailhache, editors of the *Journal*, were themselves active participants in the county and state political committees of their respective parties. The daily debate between the two papers thus provided an unusual record of the Sangamon County political climate in 1858.

While none of the seven famous Douglas-Lincoln debates of August, September, and October was held in Springfield, each man spoke there three times during the canvass. Lincoln's opening speech of the campaign was in Springfield, and its assertion that a house divided against itself could not stand, not only established the direction of the contest with Douglas, but launched Lincoln's national career. The response of the two papers to that speech and to the canvass that followed revealed how much Springfield itself was a house divided on the slavery issue and how sensitive was the attendant issue of Negro equality for Lincoln's neighbors. At the same time, in trying to moderate their own positions for this balance-wheel electorate, while exaggerating the radicalism of the other's ideas, both Lincoln and Douglas in Springfield and Sangamon County in 1858 revealed important elements of their potential for national leadership. This local listening post for the great Senate campaign thus provided both context and consequences for their battle two years later for the presidency.

Douglas's Senate speech against the Kansas policies of the Democratic president, James Buchanan, the previous December had set the stage for the 1858 Senate race in Illinois. Buchanan's effort to force a proslavery constitution on Kansas when it applied for statehood directly violated the doctrine of popular sovereignty which Douglas had made his political creed. Challenged frequently for his opportunism and lack of principle, Douglas determined to oppose the proslavery Lecompton Constitution and to uphold popular sovereignty in Kansas at whatever cost. Three days before his December Senate speech, Douglas apprized Charles Lanphier in Springfield that "We will nail our colors to the mast and defend the right of the people to govern themselves against all assaults from all quarters. We are sure to triumph." [2]

To the Republicans in Illinois, Douglas's break with the man he had helped elect president in 1856 was confounding. The Republican party had developed among old Whigs and antislavery Democrats in part as a response to Douglas's own Kansas-Nebraska Act of 1854, which overturned the Missouri Compromise and opened the territories to slavery. Abraham Lincoln himself began his emergence as a leader of this new party in a historic debate on that act with Douglas in Springfield in October, 1854.[3] Douglas's defense in June, 1857, of the Supreme Court's proslavery *Dred Scott* decision, again in Springfield, had deepened the antagonism toward him of the antislavery element which controlled the Republican party. On the other hand, his break with Buchanan in December, 1857, opposing a proslavery constitution for Kansas because it had not been secured on the basis of popular sovereignty, seemed to pull the ground from under the Republicans. One Springfield friend wrote to Douglas in early January that in traveling throughout central and southern Illinois, he had not met the first Democrat "who is not with you heart and hand." Even Republicans were "openly and enthusiastically approving" of Douglas's course.[4]

To the Douglas camp early in 1858, however, the response of Republicans was less critical than that of the Illinois Democracy. The uncompromising stand by Douglas, the independent man of the new Northwest, against James Buchanan, the old man of Pennsylvania and supporter of the slave South, could prove disastrous for Douglas and his party in Illinois. From Washington at the end of January, Maj. Thomas L. Harris, the congressman from the Sixth District, including Sangamon County, and Douglas's major ally in the House of Representatives on the Kansas question, sent his assessment of the

political realities to Lanphier in Springfield. "The Pres is determined to crush us all," Harris reported. "You must carefully prepare
things for the next campaign—The issues are those of life and death
—If we have harmony—we will have success—If any serious splits
—we are gone. . . . When the message comes—hold your breath—
Douglas will shake the Capitol & the country—"[5] To his *Register*
readers, Lanphier forecast that the struggle over the Lecompton Constitution "promises increased vexation and difficulty—probably
civil war. As a measure affecting the welfare of the democratic party,
it points to disintegration and ruin."[6]

The Republicans at the *Journal* looked on almost in disbelief.
Douglas, their long standing enemy, now provoked their grudging
admiration. If Douglas should stand firm with the Republicans, the
Journal predicted, together they could prevent Southern bullying
and "defeat the disunionists and kill off effectually the Lecompton
juggle."[7] The passage with Republican votes of Harris's resolution
to refer Buchanan's February Message on the Lecompton Constitution to a select committee of the Congress demonstrated the determination of the Douglas forces to defeat the president on Kansas.
Under the headline "The Republican Triumph in Congress—The
Beginning of the End of the Slave-holding Rule," the *Journal* took
a far-reaching view of the political upheaval set loose by Kansas.
Those Democrats like Douglas and Harris, who had taken sides
against the proslavery National Democratic party and joined with
Republicans on Kansas, would find they had committed the unpar-
donable sin. "They may organize a faction in the North," observed
the *Journal*, "but it will avail nothing. The hosts of the Republicans
will override them, and trample them. The people are too earnest
upon this great question of extending Liberty, to be thwarted or driv-
en aside by a faction." Shall free principles or slave principles prevail? That was the question. There was no middle ground. The slave
power had broken the once great Whig party, the *Journal* recalled.
"It has now done the same thing for the Democratic party."[8]

Amidst such political divisions, the *Journal* invited the anti-
Lecompton Democrats to follow the logic of their new position, as
had the anti-Nebraska Democrats four years before, and join the Republicans against the slave power which was now in full possession
of the National Democratic Party. On the other hand, the Springfield
friends of Abraham Lincoln at the *Journal*, to gain partisan advantage
over the Douglas Democrats, attended and publicized the Buchanan-

ites' activity around the state. The *Journal* reported extensively and sympathetically such proceedings of the Buchanan Democrats as their April convention, held in the Senate Chamber of the statehouse, while the Douglas Democrats were holding their state convention over in the Hall of Representatives. The *Journal* also shed crocodile tears for almost every Douglas postmaster removed from office as part of Buchanan's retaliation against Douglas. In the campaign ahead a perverse alliance emerged of antislavery Republicans with proslavery Buchanan Democrats joined against the Douglas Democrats who were determined to sidestep the issue of slavery itself as too disruptive for the safety of the Union. To many, both in Illinois and the nation, Douglas appeared to occupy the honorable middle between two unscrupulous extremes.[9]

Where was Abraham Lincoln during this period of transformation of Douglas from opportunist to man of principle? If one looks for Lincoln in the *Journal* and the *Register*, he was practically nonexistent. Except for his legal defense of Governor Bissell's veto of the reapportionment act, there was no solid mention of Lincoln politically in either paper from January until April 19, except for a March 4 reference in the *Journal* to the open declaration by Buchanan agents "that they will accept Abe Lincoln with joy, if only with him they can crush Douglas."[10] Even on April 19 in what amounted to an oblique announcement of Lincoln's candidacy, the *State Journal* quoted without comment the *Chicago Journal*'s article entitled "The Position of Senator Douglas at Home." "We are glad that the *Register* assumes such a defiant tone, and scouts the aid and assistance of Black Republicans, to return Mr. Douglas," the *Chicago Journal* exclaimed. "It will serve to open the eyes of those, if there were any in our ranks, who believed they saw signs of repentance in our Senator, and had begun to calculate the chances of his complete reformation, while it affords us an opportunity to say that the Republican party, pledged to the support of the gallant Lincoln, can in no event or manner aid or assist in the re election of Mr. Douglas."[11]

The next day, the *Register* remarked that now that its neighbor, the *Journal* (this reference and all *Journal* references hereafter are to the *Illinois State Journal*), "raises Mr. Abraham Lincoln upon its banner to succeed Senator Douglas," it was thereby taking abolition ground, thus sacrificing its appeal to the old Whigs. "Outside of Illinois," the *Register* observed, "republicanism is endeavoring to make capital from their new position. Here its leaders would do the same thing, but the process necessarily involves approval of the great champion of an 'immense good' [Douglas], and consequent marring of the personal schemes of leaders who are willing to adopt the policy and its glorious results, but who want the *place* and the honors of its greatest champion." [12] In recent weeks, the Republicans had appeared to want to share Douglas's popular sovereignty doctrine. In choosing Lincoln, suggested the *Register* in this opening shot of the campaign, the *Journal* abandoned Douglas's popular sovereignty ground and moved toward the outright abolition position of "no more slave states." The *Register*, however, did not yet concede that Lincoln would be the Republican candidate. Much more likely, it kept insisting, was "Long John" Wentworth, editor of the *Chicago Democrat* and, from the *Register's* perspective, a thorough and despicable Black Republican.[13]

Whatever its real reading of Republican politics, the *Register* did no detailed analysis of Lincoln as a man, as a candidate, or as a neighbor in the half year prior to his nomination. When coupled with the strategic silence of the *Journal*, which even after mid-April only occasionally reprinted articles in support of Lincoln from other newspapers around the state and nation, there was a curious blackout by Springfield's two major papers of the remarkable campaign being waged for the Republican Senate nomination by their fellow townsman.[14] The contrast with Douglas could not have been greater. Both the *Journal* and the *Register* repeatedly analyzed his Senate performance, his candidacy, his personal strengths and failings, his points of view, and his fitness not only for the Senate but for the presidency in 1860. In both papers, there were few days after Douglas's December, 1857, Senate speech without a reference to him, and frequently the news columns were filled with him.[15]

The situation in central Illinois on the eve of the Republican State Convention, scheduled for June 16 in Springfield, seemed extremely favorable for Stephen Douglas. Abraham Lincoln had remained quiet during the fight over the Lecompton Constitution which, with the Republicans, Douglas and Harris had defeated. Eastern Republicans expressed hopes that the valiant Douglas would be returned to the Senate to play his uniquely independent role. The *Journal* was resentful and uncomfortable at this courting of its longtime enemy, and responded by urging the Douglasites to join the Republican party, but not with Douglas as their senatorial candidate. United as

Illinoisans against the disunionist sentiment of the South and that of the most radical abolitionists in the North, the followers of Lincoln and Douglas in central Illinois seemed to occupy extensively similar ground. The national debate over Kansas had been on Douglas's terms and most people in Illinois seemed proud of the leadership demonstrated by their senior senator.[16] Along with the resolutions endorsing Lincoln for the Senate immediately prior to the convention in Springfield, many Republican county conventions in central and southern Illinois also adopted resolutions hailing Douglas's courageous battle on Kansas.[17]

Into this setting Lincoln injected his "House Divided" speech. We know from his law partner, William Herndon, how much Lincoln worked on the address and that a preliminary reading of it to a group of Springfield Republican friends won no support except that of Herndon for the radical ground Lincoln proposed to take.[18] He opened up the issue of slavery as it affected the very survival of the Union and of freemen governing themselves. While he sought to make a distinction between what he expected and what he desired in terms of the Union, Lincoln in effect rejected any illusion harbored by the victors in the Kansas battle that slavery agitation was now behind them. He charged Douglas with being a fellow conspirator with the slave power, thus seeking to reestablish with the electorate Douglas's proslavery image which had been obscured by the fight over Kansas. Out of office for almost a decade, Lincoln challenged Douglas, the leading politician in the nation, to fight on Lincoln's terms. Taking on Douglas as aggressively as Douglas had taken on Buchanan the previous December, Lincoln in his Springfield speech went to the heart of the nation's dilemma, the continued existence of slavery, an approach which Douglas's entire political future required him to skirt.

If we could first know *where* we are, and *whither* we are tending, we could then better judge *what* to do, and *how* to do it.

We are now far into the *fifth* year, since a policy was initiated, with the *avowed* object, and *confident* promise, of putting an end to slavery agitation.

Under the operation of that policy, that agitation has not only, *not ceased*, but has *constantly augmented*.

In *my* opinion, it *will* not cease, until a *crisis* shall have been reached, and passed.

A house divided against itself cannot stand.

I believe this government cannot endure, permanently half *slave* and half *free*.

I do not expect the Union to be *dissolved*—I do not expect the house to *fall*—but I *do* expect it will cease to be divided.

It will become *all* one thing, or *all* the other.

Either the *opponents* of slavery, will arrest the further spread of it, and place it where the public mind shall rest in the belief that it is in course of ultimate extinction; or its *advocates* will push it forward, till it shall become alike lawful in *all* the States, *old* as well as *new*—*North* as well as *South*.[19]

Knowing the *Journal* and the *Register* as he did, Lincoln could have had few illusions about how the press in his own city would respond. These opening lines of the speech soon became famous throughout the nation. But while they would be attacked repeatedly throughout the campaign by Douglas and by Lanphier in the *Register*, they would be all but ignored by Lincoln's friends at the *Journal*.

During the first several weeks after Lincoln's "House Divided" speech, the *Journal* and the *Register* jockeyed for position. They dealt with old battles, such as the *Register's* attack on Lincoln's Mexican "spot" resolution and the *Journal's* insistence that Douglas's Kansas-Nebraska Act in 1854 was the real source of the present agitation over slavery.[20] Each side amplified the divisions in the other's ranks. The *Journal* extensively covered the plans of the Buchananites to oppose Douglas, including a rumor that Dr. Charles Leib, one of Buchanan's henchmen in Chicago, intended "following Douglas in reply throughout the State," an interesting anticipation of the strategy Lincoln himself later employed.[21] Mindful of the Republicans' need to convert Fillmore Americans and old Whigs to their side, the *Register* attempted to put questions to the *Journal* in as embarrassing a fashion as possible to frustrate that coalition. "Does republicanism, as sustained by that party in Illinois, recognize the right of new states to come in the Union, with or without slavery, as the *people* of such states may decide?" asked the *Register*. "Will Mr. Lincoln, if he breaks into the senate, stand with Hale, Wade, Wilson & Co., or will he recognize the democratic Douglas doctrine of the right of the people to 'regulate their own domestic institutions, in their own way, subject only to the constitution of the United States?' This is the question."[22] The question-asking tactic thus prepared by the press was the same employed later in the debates between Douglas and Lincoln themselves. The Democratic *Register* suggested the answers Republicans had already given by nominating Lincoln: "1st—to arrest the further spread of slavery; 2d—its ultimate *extinction* or *abolition*."[23] The Republican *Journal*, in response, concluded that the Democratic platform under Douglas must therefore advocate just the opposite: "1st—They are in favor of the unlimited spread of slavery. 2d—They are in favor of its eternal perpetuity."[24]

To the *Register's* continuing innuendos about Lincoln's advocacy of Negro equality, the *Journal* replied with an article from the recently merged *Chicago Press and Tribune* entitled "A Word for the State Register." "When we see our contemporary [the *State Register*] indulging in diatribes upon 'negro equality,' which it suddenly asserts the Republicans are aiming to establish; when we see it giving up columns to dissertations upon amalgamation, which it declares that Republicans are endeavoring to make the social law of the land; . . . when it assails Lincoln upon grounds which it knows to be false and untenable; . . . we are ready to admit that the lessons of the past have been lavished upon it in vain, and the *Register* is incorrigible."[25] The difficulty for the *Journal* was to oppose slavery, note the inhuman abuses endured by the Negro in slavery, and stand up for liberty, while not asserting the corollary objective of giving black men the social and political rights of white men. The *Journal* went as far as it dared on this touchiest of issues early in the canvass under cover of a poem entitled "The Tocsin," the last part of which would be the most outspoken identification of Lincoln with black liberty to appear in the *Journal's* pages for the remainder of the campaign.

> Illinois! The pivot on which turns the scale
> Of Liberty's blessing or Slavery's bale,
> The eyes of a continent rest on the fight—
> The hearts of the world are warm for the right!
> Illinois! Illinois! be true to the trust,
> And trample the flag of thy foes in the dust,
> Let thy watchword be Truth—not the cry of a clan,
> Who worship the prestige and prowess of man,
> But mindful, the cause of the poor and oppressed,
> Most safely shall rest in Abraham's breast.
> O take a *link off* from the slave-chain, anon,
> And to Liberty's livery add a Lincoln.[26]

Stephen Douglas returned to the campaign in Illinois a hero, unlike his return in 1854 after introducing the Kansas-Nebraska Act, when, he recalled for a Springfield audience, he could "travel from Boston to Chicago by the light of my own effigies."[27] After opening the canvass with speeches on two successive days in Chicago, July 9 and 10, Douglas and Lincoln headed for Springfield. In response to their Chicago exchange, and the *Journal*'s coverage of it, the *Register* observed that "Lincoln is ahead of his organs in abolitionism."[28] The concluding portion of his Chicago speech particularly offended Lincoln's neighbors at the *Register*. Lincoln had declared, "Let us discard all this quibbling about this man and the other man—this race and that race and the other race being inferior, and therefore they must be placed in an inferior position—discarding our standard that we have left us. Let us discard all these things, and unite as one people throughout this land, until we shall once more stand up declaring that all men are created equal."[29] The *Register* hereafter linked this paragraph with the opening of the "House Divided" speech to demonstrate Lincoln's out-and-out abolitionism and belief in Negro equality. From the perspective of his Democratic enemies at the *Register*, Lincoln spent the rest of the campaign attempting to counteract the negative reactions to these two early "radical" pronouncements. In response to the *Register*'s attack, the *Journal* sought at first to ignore the charges of Lincoln's abolitionism and belief in Negro equality and then awkwardly attempted to deny such charges.

Taking the offensive, the *Journal* thought Douglas's trip reminiscent of many other pilgrimages to Springfield, from his support of the Missouri Compromise in 1848, to his defense of its overthrow by his Kansas-Nebraska Act in 1854, to his defense of the *Dred Scott* decision with its overthrow of popular sovereignty in 1857. "Down he is to come on Saturday to the theatre whereon he has heretofore exhibited his inconsistences, his contradictions, and thrown his sommersaults," the *Journal* announced.[30]

In Edwards Grove, on July 17, Douglas delivered a stirring defense of his fight against the Lecompton swindle, including his standing side by side with Republicans—or their standing side by side with him. He turned to Lincoln's "House Divided" speech and asked by what means his opponent was going to make all the states free. "All he proposes," Douglas explained, "is to invite the people of Illinois and every other free state to band together as one sectional party, governed and divided by a geographical line, to make war upon the institution of slavery in the slaveholding states. He is going to carry it out by means of a political party, that has its adherents only in the free states; a political party, that does not pretend that it can give [sic] a solitary vote in the slave states of the Union, and by this sectional vote he is going to elect a president of the United States, form a cabinet and administer the government on sectional grounds, being the power of the north over that of the south. In other words, he invites a war of the north against the south, a warfare of the free states against the slaveholding states." Douglas then moved to Lincoln's attack on the Supreme Court's *Dred Scott* decision and asked how Lincoln, a lawyer, proposed to reverse it. "When we refuse to abide by judicial decisions what protection is there left for life and property? To whom shall you appeal? To mob law, to partisan caucuses, to town meetings, to revolution?" Douglas thundered.

He saved till last what he charged was Lincoln's main objection to the *Dred Scott* decision. "His principal objection to that decision," Douglas explained, "is that it was intended to deprive the negro of the rights of citizenship in the different states of the Union. Well, suppose it was, and there is no doubt that that was its legal effect, what is his objection to it? Why, he thinks that a negro ought to be permitted to have the rights of citizenship. . . . Here I have a direct issue with Mr. Lincoln. I am not in favor of negro citizenship. ('Nor I,' responded the crowd, 'Hurrah for Douglas,' 'good, good,' &c.) I do not believe that a negro is a citizen or ought to be a citizen. ('Hurrah for Douglas.') I believe that this government of ours was founded and wisely founded, upon the white basis. ('That's right,' 'Hurrah,' 'Bravo,' &c.) It was made by white men for the benefit of white men and their posterity, to be executed and managed by white men. ('Glory to you,' 'Hurrah for Douglas,' and great applause.)"[31]

Lincoln did not hear Douglas's speech but had listened to his address in Bloomington on the way down to Springfield and guessed he knew what the judge would say. That night at the statehouse, Lincoln responded. The speech for this hometown gathering reads like a legal brief, closely testing Douglas's use of evidence. Acknowledging the political disabilities faced by the Republicans with a malapportioned legislature and the "world wide renown" of Senator Douglas, whom many expected soon to be president, Lincoln expressed his frustration that Douglas had increased these obstacles by determining purposely to misrepresent Lincoln's earlier speech in Springfield. The staple of Douglas's campaign was "popular sovereignty" and Lincoln examined it as it applied to Negro slavery, the only real question Lincoln believed to be at issue. When Douglas talked about devoting his life to popular sovereignty, Lincoln asked, does he mean to secure to people in the territories the right to exclude slavery from the territories? "If he means so to say, he means to deceive; because he and every one knows that the decision of the Supreme Court, which he approves and makes especial ground of attack upon me for disapproving, forbids the people of a territory to exclude slavery." No one disagreed on the principle of popular sovereignty, Lincoln asserted. The dispute over the Lecompton Constitution related to the fact of whether it "had been fairly formed by the people or not." Douglas and the Republicans were on one side, the president and his allies on the other in judging the facts, not the principle. Lincoln described Douglas's doctrine of popular sovereignty as "the most errant humbug that has ever been attempted on an intelligent community." He spurned Douglas's professional attacks on him as a lawyer for objecting to the *Dred Scott* decision. "It so happens, singularly enough, that I never stood opposed to a decision of the Supreme Court till this," Lincoln declared. "On the contrary, I have no recollection that he was ever particularly in favor of one till this," and this decision aimed to nationalize slavery.

Furthermore, despite his ostensible horror at Lincoln's disposition to make Negroes perfectly equal with white men in social and political relations, Douglas had not stopped to show that Lincoln had ever said such a thing, "or that it legitimately follows from any thing I have said, but he rushes on with his assertions." If Douglas and his friends did not, as he did, adhere to the Declaration of Independence as stated, retorted Lincoln, "Let them make it read that all men are created equal except negroes." If not equal in color, the Negro was the white man's equal in his right to life, liberty, and the pursuit of happiness. "All I ask for the negro is that if you do not like him, let him alone. If God gave him but little, that little let him enjoy." Finally, in spite of Douglas's assertions that he had read Lincoln's June 16 speech carefully, with its charge that he was a party to a conspiracy to nationalize slavery, Douglas had not yet contradicted the charge. "On his own tacit admission," Lincoln declared, "I renew that charge."[32]

The *Journal* praised Lincoln's speech for demolishing Douglas. Lincoln's "onslaught was terrible," his friends exclaimed. But again, as after June 16, there was no elucidation by the *Journal* of his stand on the issue of Negro equality.[33] Predictably, for the *Register*, that issue provided the inspiration for a continuing commentary over more than a week. It discerned a regional strategy at work in Lincoln's campaign. His first Springfield speech, accepting the nomination, and his Chicago speech of July 10 were abolitionist, directed to his Northern audience. "Mr. Lincoln dared not repeat, on Saturday last, the same doctrine to his old whig friends of Sangamon—the old Henry Clay whigs—the Kentuckians and Tennessans [sic] of central Illinois, so that he tried on that occasion to make it appear that he did not mean what he said in the republican convention."[34] The *Register* had nothing but contempt for Lincoln's narrow use of popular sovereignty to apply only to Negro slavery. With Lincoln, "the question of slavery is, as he says, the '*paramount*' question . . . in the whole of this speech, no allusion is made to the interests of the *white man*. . . . Slavery, the negro, this is the 'paramount question.'"[35] To counter Lincoln's argument against Douglas of being a party to a conspiracy to nationalize slavery, the *Register* charged Lincoln with wanting to go to the Senate "for the sole object, again by congressional interference, to raise the storm of slavery agitation."[36] The *Register* doubted that "the white men of the prairie state" would submit to the amalgamation theories implicit in Lincoln's argument which Lanphier expressed in a syllogism: "The negro is a man; the declaration of independence says 'that all men are created equal,' consequently the negro is equal with the white man."[37]

The *Journal*'s response to the *Register*'s aggressive attack on Lincoln's abolitionism was at times tortured. While the *Journal*, like Lincoln, was unequivocally opposed to the extension of slavery, like Lincoln, it also felt called upon to reiterate its commitment not to disturb slavery where it existed. On the issue of Negro equality, the *Journal* editors squirmed. One example revealed their dilemma. On August 7, the *Register* reported a speech at Poughkeepsie, New York, by Frederick Douglass, under the title "Another Ally of Lincoln—The Nigger Chief Out for Him," in which Frederick Douglass criticized Stephen Douglas and praised Lincoln, hailing the "House Divided" speech as the "keynote of republicanism" in Illinois.[38] To demonstrate their white credentials and in apparent response to their neighbor's repeated badgering to acknowledge the Douglass speech, the *Journal* editors finally took note of the *Register*'s grief over "Fred" Douglass's opposition to "Steve" Douglas. "That sheet may now console itself," the *Journal* advised. "We see by the Springfield *State Democrat* [the Buchanan newspaper in Springfield] that, at Mr. Douglas' Edwardsville ovation, 'a big buck nigger brought up the procession, and hurrahed for Mr. Douglas at the top of his voice.' It says there was likewise 'a nigger show' on the grounds where Mr. Douglas spoke."[39] Thus did the *Journal* deal with the embarrassment of Lincoln's being praised by the leading black spokesman in the country.

Discovering a pro-Douglas paper in Northern Illinois, the *DeKalb County Sentinel*, which frankly favored the equality of blacks with whites, the *Journal* sought to turn Douglas's own weapons against him by charging him with a "change of principles for each degree of latitude . . . from advocacy of negro slavery in Southern Illinois to negro equality in the North; from the nationalization of slavery here to practical amalgamation in DeKalb County." Douglas would find, the *Journal* unctuously warned, "that both doctrines are equally disgusting and abhorrent to the people of Illinois . . . that the people are as opposed to negro equality and amalgamation as they are to Dred Scottism and the nationalization of slavery in all the States and Territories. They will stand, with Mr. Lincoln and the Republican party, on the white man's platform, which leaves slavery where it has rights by law, and is in favor of reserving the Territories to the free and untrammelled industry and enterprise of white men."[40] In its defensiveness, the *Journal* pot thus called the *Register* kettle black.

On the stump, Lincoln bore in on the contradiction between Douglas's doctrine of popular sovereignty and the *Dred Scott* decision, with its guarantee that slavery could be carried into any state, regardless of popular sentiment. Under the title "Douglas Playing Double," the *Journal* reported that Douglas "finds that Lincoln is pressing home upon him with terrible effect the plain truth that Judge Taney, whom he has hitherto unqualifiedly indorsed, has completely strangled his own squatter sovereignty bantling. Afraid to change front before the enemy, he resorts to private intimations to his particular friends that the Taney doctrines most insised [sic] on by the Buchanan Democracy will have to be given over to the mercy of the Republicans. Dare he come out openly on this platform?"[41]

As Douglas prepared for the first of the seven scheduled debates with Lincoln, he wrote to Lanphier asking for information on resolutions adopted at Republican conventions held in 1854 and 1856, including Lincoln's relationship to them. "Please consult major Harris, hunt up the facts and write to me instantly directed to Ottawa,"

Douglas urged. "I must have it before next Saturday."[42] Using this information at the very outset of the first debate at Ottawa, Douglas charged Lincoln with abolitionizing the Whig party as early as 1854. Citing strong antislavery resolutions allegedly passed at the first Black Republican State Convention in Springfield in October of that year, Douglas repeated the resolutions and asked Lincoln whether he still stood pledged to them. "I desire to know," Douglas announced, "whether Mr. Lincoln's principles will bear transplanting from Ottawa to Jonesboro?"[43] Taken aback by this opening tactic, Lincoln claimed never to have had anything to do with the resolutions or the convention, although he admitted his friend Lovejoy "tried to get me into it, and I would not go in."[44] He did not at Ottawa answer Douglas's questions directly but indicated he would if the judge would reciprocate by answering questions Lincoln put to him. This initiation of direct interrogation and response on the subject of the 1854 Springfield resolutions by Douglas thus prepared the way for the questions put by Lincoln in the second debate at Freeport, demonstrating the contradiction between the Dred Scott decision and the doctrine of popular sovereignty, a connection Lincoln had been as determined to fix in the public mind as Douglas had been trying to connect Lincoln with abolitionism and Negro equality. Douglas's crucial answers to these questions were among the great consequences of the debate for Douglas's position in the country, particularly in the South.[45] The controversy over the resolutions continued throughout the campaign, leading not only to a war between the Journal and the Register but to an uncharacteristic public rebuke of Lanphier and Harris by Lincoln. At Galesburg, Lincoln pointed to the motive for what he described as their "forgery" and how the tactic was of a piece with Douglas's whole campaign "to fix extreme Abolitionism upon me."[46]

Both the historical circumstances of 1854 dredged up by Douglas and the Register and Lincoln's handling of them underscored the fine line he had walked over the past four years to keep his antislavery position from becoming outright abolitionism. During the campaign, Douglas's strategy was to force Lincoln out in the open to own up to the clear abolitionist logic of his and his party's position, and to make clear that the abolitionist logic led to sectional warfare. Nowhere was the abolitionist charge, including its corollary of Negro equality, apparently more damaging than with Lincoln's old Whig friends in Sangamon. The Register covered their defection from Lincoln with glee.[47] Under the title "Lincoln Skulks in Sanga-mon," the Register commented upon the strange front presented in his own county by Lincoln's candidates for the legislature refusing in public meetings "to acknowledge that he is their choice. . . . This is Lincoln in Sangamon!"[48]

The last weeks of the campaign in Springfield were dominated by the question of whom Henry Clay would have voted for, Douglas or Lincoln, were he still alive. Each side claimed the famous Kentucki-an's posthumous endorsement. Douglas and the Register repeatedly quoted Clay's abhorrence of abolitionism and Lincoln and the Jour-nal reiterated Clay's hope that slavery would not be extended an-other inch. The final days saw an unrelenting attack upon Lincoln. An unsigned pamphlet, entitled Lincoln and His Doctrines, began circulating around the state sometime before October 18 to show the full scope of Lincoln's belief in Negro equality and abolitionism. All the Journal could do was to sputter in frustration.[49] Douglas in his final rally in Springfield on October 20 sought to prove Lincoln's traitorous desertion of Henry Clay in 1847 and to show that Lincoln and Seward in 1850 had fomented the sectional strife which Clay and Douglas had sought to arrest.[50] The Register demonstrated that the popular Kentuckian, Senator J. J. Crittenden, the embodiment of Henry Clay's principles, was in fact for Douglas, contrary to the impression Lincoln and the Journal sought to create.[51] Other men of the South were returning to Douglas's side after his break with Buchanan, reported the Register. "These men of the south, like Douglas, are national in their ideas, and feel a deep interest in the preservation of the Union from the assaults of sectional bigots. They are not like the republicans, engaged in sectional agitation, and whose love of country only tends so far and no further."[52]

Starting on October 21 the Journal prepared to welcome Lincoln home on October 30, by running a broadside-type announcement of the rally each day in the first column of the major news page calling upon "Old Whigs of Sangamon, Will You Not Turn Out And give your old CHAMPION, ABE LINCOLN, the 'tall sucker,' a hearing for yourselves. Hear him, and you will be satisfied that the charge of NIGGER EQUALITY is as false against LINCOLN, as the charge of Toryism and Abolitionism was against CLAY!"[53] Even more reveal-ing of the Journal's defensiveness was the appearance on October 30, the day of Lincoln's rally, and on November 1, the day before the election, of a four-column spread on the front page with a two-column banner headline, "THE VIEWS AND SENTIMENTS OF HENRY CLAY AND ABE LINCOLN, ON THE SLAVERY QUESTION." Side by side, the two men's views were spelled out under such headings as "THE ABSTRACT IDEA OF EQUALITY," "THE PRACTICAL APPLICATION" of equality, "LINCOLN AND CLAY ON AMALGAMATION," "THE SEPARATION OF THE RACES," "The Ultimate Extinction of Slavery," "Lincoln Stands on the Old Whig Platform," and "Lincoln on the 'Equality' of the Races," quoting his Charleston speech of September 18, the most extensive denial during the campaign that Lincoln believed in social and political equality for blacks and whites. In the same issue, the *Journal* complained of the Democrats' charges that the Republicans and their allies were all abolitionists and in favor of the equality of Negroes with whites. "Such charges have formed the beginning, middle and ending of all the speeches made by Douglas and his satellites during the whole campaign."[54]

Lincoln's final speech was not reprinted in the *Journal*, but from one fragment that survives, Lincoln appears to have been dejected because of the misrepresentations of his feelings toward the Constitution, toward the Southern people, toward slavery, toward the Union. "Myself, and those with whom I act have been constantly accused of a purpose to destroy the union; and bespattered with every imaginable odious epithet; and some who were friends, as it were but yesterday have made themselves most active in this." While he claimed no insensibility to political honors, he affirmed that "could the Missouri restriction be restored, and the whole slavery question replaced on the old ground of 'toleration['] by *necessity* where it exists, with unyielding hostility to the spread of it, on principle, I would, in consideration, gladly agree, that Judge Douglas should never be *out*, and I never *in*, an office, so long as we both or either, live."[55]

On election day, Sangamon County went for Douglas, with a combined total for the two Douglas legislative candidates of 195 votes more than for the two Republicans. The *Register* was jubilant. "After twenty-five years spent in a minority the gallant democracy of old Sangamon, the whig citadel, takes position among the democratic counties of the state. Sangamon repudiates Lincoln and his abolitionism! Sangamon cannot be abolitionized. Recreant to his principles as a national whig, Sangamon refuses to sustain Lincoln in the odious doctrines and policy of which he has been made leader."[56] A few days later, with statewide returns slowly coming in, the *Journal* ruefully noted that "the loss to us of Madison and Sangamon counties has probably secured the re election of Senator Douglas."[57] The *Journal's* estimate was correct. When the legislature met, the switch of five House and Senate votes in these two counties from Whig or Republican to Democrat gave Douglas his margin of victory, 54 to 46. Lincoln's popular vote majority statewide was more than 4,000. Wentworth's *Chicago Democrat*, quoted in the *Journal*, commented on the critical loss of Whig support in central Illinois: "Thus was Lincoln slain in old Kentucky."[58]

According to the *Chicago Times*, Douglas's main organ in northern Illinois, no man was more responsible for defeating Lincoln than Charles Lanphier: "We know that we speak but the universal sentiment of the party in Illinois," wrote *Times* editor James Shehan, "when we say that to Charles H. Lanphier, editor of the *State Register*, is due, more than to any other man, the honor of accomplishing the great triumph in the State. Through the columns of his paper, in the preparation and distribution of documents, in visiting personally every precinct, and almost every voter in Sangamon and adjoining counties, he roused the democratic masses to a sense of the importance of the pending contest . . . the democracy of Illinois should remember the man to whom they owe so much."[59]

To account for Lanphier's unyielding hostility to Lincoln, beyond the factor of his deep personal and political loyalty to Douglas, one needs to emphasize Lanphier's apparently sincere belief that Lincoln posed a real threat to the Union. Lanphier's analysis of Lincoln in the *Register*, more than a month after the delivery of the "House Divided" speech, underscored the threat. How did Lincoln expect slavery to be abolished in the states where it legally existed, Lanphier asked, "except that, by unceasing warfare to be waged by himself and his associates in behalf of of [sic] the negro, they shall succeed in accomplishing the *extinction* of slavery in the slave states, or the 'house' shall no longer 'stand.' That his wishes are that all should be free he cannot deny. . . . Mr. Lincoln's sincerity in the opinions he puts forth in relation to the 'extinction' of slavery, and the rights of the 'negro,' makes him all the more dangerous. How easy it is for a man of his ardent temperament, who starts with an 'expectation' of a certain result, and who zealously labors to obtain the victory for his own views, to *desire* and *strive* for the *result*, when he perceives his own failure. The 'expectation' that this government cannot endure half slave and half free cannot exist in a mind like that of Mr. Lincoln, unless accompanied by the belief that it *ought not* so to exist."[60]

In the last analysis, Lincoln challenged Douglas to take a stand on slavery itself, a challenge both Douglas and Lanphier discredited and sought to evade. Beyond the moral dimensions of the challenge, clarification by Douglas of his position was politically untenable. Any suggestion that slavery should ultimately be extinguished was utterly unacceptable to Southern Democrats whom Douglas needed for the presidential contest in 1860. On the other hand, any suggestion that the expansion of slavery into the territories ought to be guaranteed by the federal government, which Southerners were demanding, was utterly unacceptable to free-soil opinion in the North. In defining this dilemma in terms of a house which would cease to be divided only when it was either all slave or all free, Lincoln forced Douglas onto ground that made his role as a unifier of Northern and Southern Democrats all but impossible. The objective was finally accomplished in the second debate at Freeport where Lincoln pressed Douglas to acknowledge that popular sovereignty and the *Dred Scott* decision were incompatible. Douglas's concession to free-soil opinion was to affirm the right of a people in a state to deny local police protection to slavery, thus circumventing the Supreme Court's guarantee that slavery could be carried into any state. Within the context of their long-standing political rivalry and the sharply contested Senate contest of 1858, Lincoln and Douglas exaggerated each other's positions and thereby strengthened the public's sense of the difficulties the nation faced in trying to compromise the issues surrounding slavery.

The Negrophobia used by Douglas and Lanphier against Lincoln can be seen as a tactical diversion from the unrelenting abolitionist logic of Lincoln's analysis. To keep from dealing head-on with slavery itself, Douglas and Lanphier almost daily appealed to whites' fear of blacks and to fears that Lincoln's hostility to slavery meant abolitionism, and abolitionism meant civil war. In central Illinois their appeal worked. But the victory for Douglas was expensive. The limits of his national strength had been carefully established by Lincoln's campaign. Down deep, that accomplishment seemed to have been grasped by Lanphier and helps account for the fury of his attacks on Lincoln which were apparently so telling with Lincoln's Whig neighbors.

That an old Kentucky Whig like Lincoln had announced from central Illinois his own calculating yet cautious estimate of the inevitability of a crisis over slavery seemed to indicate the approach of that crisis. That he so resourcefully undermined Douglas's national position, which even Eastern Republicans had thought worth preserving, revealed Lincoln's toughness, talent, and ambition. That he took a position on the most controversial issue of the day well in advance of the views of his neighbors in Sangamon County demonstrated his intellectual independence; it also indicated his belief in the role political leaders should assume if they would lead a self-governing people. In the late 1840s he had apparently killed his political career during his one term in Congress by opposing President Polk on the Mexican War, a stand deeply unpopular in Sangamon. Now, in the late 1850s, he defeated himself among his neighbors by his controversial views on human slavery. But this time, his unpopular views at home appealed to a national constituency beyond Springfield from whom within days of the news of his defeat by Douglas the call began to come for Lincoln to be the Republican presidential candidate in 1860.[61] Lincoln's understanding of the divisions in the country was undoubtedly affected by the example of his own community which was itself a house divided. Two years later, a nation on the brink of civil war chose Lincoln over Douglas for president. While the South abandoned Douglas and the North selected Lincoln, the Tall Sucker's neighbors split down the middle. Springfield by a narrow margin went for Lincoln, while Sangamon County narrowly went for Douglas.

EIGHT

Lincoln and the Constitution

DON E. FEHRENBACHER

The secret of great government, Victor Hugo declared, consists in knowing precisely how much of the future can be introduced into the present. By this measure, as well as by numerous others, the Constitution of the United States is one of the supreme achievements in the history of government. Its strength and utility after nearly two centuries testify to the wisdom of the men who framed it, and in some degree to their capacity for introducing the future into the present.

Nevertheless, any reading of *The Federalist Papers*, which were in part an effort to predict how the Constitution would work in practice, will disclose evidence that the Founding Fathers did not always penetrate the distant future in construing their handiwork. James Madison, for instance, assured the people that state governments would in every respect "have the advantage of the federal government," because they would possess more power, command more popular support, and collectively employ many more persons. He also said that in a republican government, the legislative branch was bound to predominate and therefore constituted the principal threat of usurpation. Alexander Hamilton agreed, explaining that the primary reason for creation of the veto power was not to improve the quality of legislation but rather to provide the president with a means of defending himself against legislative encroachments on his authority. It was Madison who predicted that the House of Representatives would be more powerful than the Senate; and it was Hamilton who characterized the judiciary as "beyond comparison the weakest of the three departments of power," having "no direction either of the strength or of the wealth of the society," and able to take "no active resolution whatever." But the passage likely to inspire the bitterest smiles in the 1970s is one in which Hamilton discussed the kind of person who would occupy the presidency:

This process of election affords a moral certainty that the office of President will seldom fall to the lot of any man who is not in an eminent degree endowed with the requisite qualifications. Talents for low intrigue, and the little arts of popularity, may alone suffice to elevate a man to the first honors in a single State; but it will require other talents, and a different kind of merit, to establish him in the esteem and confidence of the whole Union. . . . It will not be too strong to say that there will be a constant probability of seeing the station filled by characters pre-eminent for ability and virtue.[1]

If Madison, Hamilton, and the other framers could be reconvened to inspect the modern version of the constitutional system created in 1787, they would find it reassuringly familiar on paper but fearfully different in operation. Of all the changes catching their bewildered attention, three would be especially conspicuous—the extraordinary shift of responsibility and authority from the states to the central government; the vast increase in the power of the presidency and in the range of executive functions; and the astonishingly active, even aggressive role now assumed by the judiciary in the determination of public policy. All three of these revolutionary changes in the structure of the American republic took place over long periods of time and can be attributed to no single event, not even an event as momentous as the Civil War. Yet one may appropriately ask the extent to which the process of change in each case was accelerated or retarded by the Civil War and in what manner that process was affected by the character, purposes, and conduct of Abraham Lincoln.

According to the set of answers that until recently would have been returned by the legendary creature known as "any schoolboy," the Civil War greatly stimulated the progress of national consolidation and the growth of presidential power, but it further eroded the prestige and authority of a Supreme Court already weakened by the "self-inflicted wound" of the Dred Scott decision. To say that these generalizations are inadequate and therefore misleading is not the same as declaring that they are wrong. Since historical truth is usually complex, and half-truth may sometimes be more harmful than outright error, the historian's most delicate task, and perhaps his most important responsibility, is the work of refining and qualifying generalizations, including his own.

The Civil War did confirm the indestructibility of the American Union, and it did fix the primary locus of sovereignty in the nation, rather than in the several states. Secession, like slavery, was buried at Appomattox, together with the discredited constitutional doctrines of John C. Calhoun. Nationalism thus triumphed in the outcome of the conflict, but long before that day arrived, the conduct of the war had necessitated a great expansion in the responsibilities and authority of the federal government. One case in point is the raising of troops, which at first was managed almost entirely by the state governments but gradually came under federal control, with the states reduced to serving virtually as administrative units in the maintenance of a national army. Similarly, the financial necessities of war compelled the creation of a national banking system to supplement and partly replace the jumble of state banks with their multitudinous currencies. Secession facilitated this and other important legislation by removing from Congress the very elements that had always been most hostile to the expansion of federal power. Meanwhile, the mobilizing armies had become "enormous forcing rooms for the quick flowering of nationalistic feeling,"[2] and civilians were not far behind soldiers in realizing how much more closely the war had bound their lives and hopes to the nation.

Abraham Lincoln presided over this movement toward national consolidation without displaying any serious misgivings about it. His outlook, unlike his background, had never been parochial. His one passion, as Walt Whitman observed, was for the federal Union. He paid due respect to the principle of States' Rights but insisted that no state except Texas during its decade of independence had ever been a sovereignty. His most emphatic pronouncement on the subject was made as president-elect in the form of a rhetorical question put to an Indiana audience: "If a State, in one instance, and a county in another, should be equal in extent of territory, and equal in the number of people, wherein is that State any better than the county?"[3] And on that memorable day at Gettysburg in November, 1863, he said nothing about the states but spoke only of the nation— the nation conceived in liberty and dedicated to the principle that men are born equal, the nation undergoing the supreme test of civil war, the nation destined to have a new birth of freedom. It is scarcely surprising that Lincoln, the Great Emancipator, should also have been widely regarded as the great symbol of democratic nationalism, and therefore as an opponent of the particularism and strict constitutionalism usually associated with States' Rights. He headed a political party, said Alexander H. Stephens shortly after Appomattox, that "virtually hoisted the banner of Consolidation" in a war fought primarily, not against slavery, but against the principle of federalism. Echoing this judgment nearly a hundred years later, the Civil War scholar William B. Hesseltine declared that Lincoln was a revolutionary leader who deliberately "destroyed the rights and powers of the states" in order to erect "a sovereign and centralized nation."[4]

Yet, on closer scrutiny, one is struck by the limited and, in many respects, temporary character of this alleged revolution, and by the tenacity with which federalism survived the war and its aftermath. The North fought for the purpose of canceling secession and blotting the Southern Confederacy out of existence. It would have been logical to obliterate also the agencies that had enacted secession and created the Confederacy. But except for the partition of Virginia, a very special case, the integrity of the rebellious states was never seriously threatened. Proposals for reducing them to the status of federal territories, although seriously discussed, got nowhere in Congress. The slaves of the Confederacy were emancipated; much of its private property was confiscated or destroyed; its leaders were disfranchised and otherwise punished; but the Confederate states retained their identities and became in time the principal agencies for preserving and elaborating the legend of the Lost Cause.

Lincoln's program of Reconstruction was designed to restore the seceded states quickly and easily to their former places in the Union. Often praised for its magnanimity, it nevertheless neglected the problems and needs of four million liberated slaves, whose best hope lay in the continued exertion of federal power for their aid and protection. Lincoln's plan would have put the freedman promptly where he was destined to end up eventually—that is, under the domination of white Southerners who held firm control of their state and local governments—but with the important difference that there would have been no Fourteenth and Fifteenth amendments to carry the promise of a better future.

Historians have offered various explanations of Lincoln's attitude toward Reconstruction. For one thing, vindictiveness was simply alien to his nature, and in any case he believed that generous treatment of the South would be sound policy, promoting the spirit of reconciliation necessary for true reunion. Perhaps he also intended that his strategy should lay the foundation for an effective Republican party in the South. Furthermore, he feared eruptions of anarchy and violence when the Confederacy was overthrown and thought that an early restoration of normal civil government would be the best preventive. According to some critics, the lack of sufficient concern for the freedman in his program reflected the common racist assumption that America was a white man's country. It has also been suggested that an uneasy sense of personal responsibility for starting the war made him especially anxious for a speedy restoration of the Union on lenient terms. In addition, Lincoln's Reconstruction policy of treating the Southern states as though they had never left the Union followed consistently the official Lincolnian theory on the nature of the war, which held that secession was illegal, the Confederacy a fiction, and the federal Union accordingly still intact.

To these explanations, whatever their value may be, at least one more should be added, and that is Lincoln's essentially traditional conception of the Republic he was trying to save. The Civil War may have had revolutionary effects, but it was begun and prosecuted for conservative purposes—to preserve the Union on one side, to protect slavery on the other. Emancipation, for example, was the revolutionary purpose of only a small abolitionist minority; for most Americans it emerged as a revolutionary consequence of disunion and war. Lincoln and other Northerners, out of their own experience, could nevertheless readily envision a Union restored without slavery, and Southern people, too, realized long before Appomattox that emancipation would be one of the penalties exacted if the Confederacy should fail. But nowhere in either North or South was there reason to expect, or even the capacity to visualize, a Union reconstructed on any basis except the old system of federalism, with its familiar distribution of responsibilities and powers.

Under that system, most of the governmental activity affecting the daily lives of ordinary citizens (not less than 90 percent, according to one contemporary estimate) was carried on by the states and their subdivisions.[5] Thus when Lincoln, during the senatorial campaign with Douglas in 1858, found himself persistently accused of favoring racial equality, he made this reply: "I do not understand there is any place where an alteration of the social and political relations of the negro and the white man can be made except in the State Legislature —not in the Congress of the United States."[6] Seven years later, in the closing days of the war, his outlook on race relations continued to be guided and restricted by his traditional view of federal relations. For instance, he had already come to favor and recommend some measure of Negro suffrage, but he was unwilling to have it imposed on the Southern states as a condition of their restoration. It appears, then, that in spite of his cavalier reference to the states as little better than oversized counties, Lincoln's policy-making reflected the orthodox conception of the United States as a relatively decentralized federation in which the state governments played the most active and versatile part.

During the period of Radical Reconstruction that began in the late 1860s, the federal government did, of course, use its civil and military power to compel enfranchisement of the freedman and to lend him certain other kinds of protection. That effort, however, remained vigorous for no more than a decade. By the 1890s, it had come to an end completely, with the Southern Negro secure once again in the iron grip of white supremacy. The overthrow of Radical Reconstruction used to be explained as a popular reaction against partisan, vindictive policies that had become increasingly corrupt in operation. More recently, it has been interpreted as a failure of justice, made more or less inevitable by the racism that infected most white Americans, in the North as well as in the South. Still more recently, some historians have argued that constitutional inhibitions may have been the critical factor. That is, the amount of federal intervention needed to sustain Radical Reconstruction simply could not be squared with the traditional American conception of the structure of the Republic. "Respect for federalism," says one of these scholars, was "the most potent institutional obstacle to the Negroes' hope for protected liberty."[7]

When one turns from Reconstruction itself to other governmental activity of the same period, the centralizing influence of the Civil War becomes no easier to assess. The scope of national legislation expanded considerably, but so too did the scope of state legislation, and any shift in the balance of federalism was a modest one at most. The federal government increased its control over banking and currency after the war, but relinquished its wartime authority over the railroads. Railroad legislation, although badly needed, remained in the hands of the states until a Supreme Court decision virtually compelled passage of the Interstate Commerce Act in 1887. That statute marked the beginning of a new era in which federal power was used extensively for regulatory and police purposes. Populist-Progressive reform may have drawn some strength from the Civil War precedent of vigorous federal action, but otherwise there was not much continuity between those two surges of national effort. In general, then the amount of permanent consolidation produced by the war seems neither small enough to be called unimportant nor large enough to be called revolutionary. The principal achievement for American nationalism under Lincoln's leadership was the negative one of arresting a drift toward decentralization that had become a plunge into disintegration.

The expansion of federal power during the Civil War was closely associated with an expansion of executive power within the federal government. On this latter subject, it appears easy to speak unequivocally; for most historians agree with the statement of Clinton Rossiter that Lincoln "pushed the powers of the Presidency to a new plateau high above any conception of executive authority hitherto imagined in this country." Samuel Eliot Morison said that he "came near to being the ideal tyrant of whom Plato dreamed," and Lord Bryce, in *The American Commonwealth*, compared him to a Roman dictator.[8] In fact, serious scholars have applied the word "dictator" more often to Lincoln than to any other president. The list of his presidential actions inspiring such judgments is a rather long one. With Congress, by his own arrangement, not in session, he responded to the attack on Fort Sumter by enlarging the army, proclaiming a blockade of Southern ports, suspending the writ of habeas corpus in certain areas, authorizing arbitrary arrests and imprisonments on a large scale, and spending public funds without legal warrant. He never yielded the initiative seized at this time, and, in later bold assertions of executive authority, he introduced conscription, proclaimed emancipation, and inaugurated a program of reconstruction.

But David Donald reminds us that Lincoln was also in some ways a passive president, one who displayed little legislative leadership and exercised surprisingly little control over his department heads; who vetoed only one major piece of legislation and deferred humbly to members of Congress in making his appointments. The explanation, according to Donald, is that Lincoln played almost to perfection the role of a "Whig in the White House."[9] The American Whigs, taking their name from opponents of the royal prerogative in England, had originated as the party of resistance to the "executive tyranny" of Andrew Jackson, whom they sometimes called "King Andrew the First." Thus, without denying the need for vigorous executive leadership in the prosecution of a war, the Whigs maintained that Congress was the proper source of governmental initiative, and that the president should play no part in the lawmaking process except to implement the legislative will. Lincoln, as president-elect, reaffirmed his adherence to this principle, and it no doubt had some influence on his performance in office. It could be argued, of course, that Lincoln's presidential style was shaped less by a devotion to Whig political theory than by a single-minded determination to win the war. But whatever the reason for it, a curious dualism does run through his use of executive authority. The record suggests that if he had served at a more normal time, his performance in the White House might have been relatively subdued. As it was, he set a precedent for immense expansion of presidential power—presumably applicable, however, only in a state of extreme emergency.

Lincoln believed that the power needed to meet the secession crisis had been provided by the Constitution and vested primarily in the president. He cited the commander-in-chief clause, the clause requiring him to "take care that the laws be faithfully executed," and his presidential oath—"registered in heaven," as he put it—to "preserve, protect and defend the Constitution of the United States." Quite obviously, this emergency power had to be sufficient for the occasion or else it would be useless. Thus the extent of the power depended on the character and magnitude of the emergency, which in turn, because of the nature of presidential responsibility, could be determined only by the president himself.

Not even a universal acceptance of this remarkable argument would have been conclusive, however; for every federal action must pass *two* constitutional tests. The first is whether the Constitution authorizes it; the second is whether the Constitution forbids it. Certain practices of the Lincoln administration plainly conflicted with some of the most cherished clauses in the Bill of Rights. To be sure, the perilous circumstances called for extraordinary measures, and the intent of even the most repressive actions was preventive rather than punitive. Nevertheless, the secret police, paid informers, midnight arrests, crowded prisons, and suppressed newspapers were alien to the American experience, and this most abused of presidents suffered his worst abuse as the alleged assassin of his country's freedom.

Lincoln's eloquent defense proceeded from the assumption that individual freedom is secure only in a self-governing society. To him, it was a matter of temporarily diminishing the rights of some persons in order to preserve an entire structure of freedom. That structure included not only the Constitution but also the functioning federal Republic that made the Constitution a reality and embodied the principle of self-government. All of this was at stake in the war. It would be folly, Lincoln maintained, to sacrifice the structure as a whole while jealously guarding some part of it. "Are all the laws, but one, to go unexecuted," he asked, "and the government itself go to pieces, lest that one be violated?" [10]

With such argument Lincoln justified emergency executive power, which he was the first American president to employ on a significant and sustained basis. The concept has roots in the practices of the Roman republic and is embraced by political philosophers as far apart in their points of view as Machiavelli and Thomas Jefferson. The highest duty of a public officer, Jefferson said, was not strict observance of the written laws but preservation of the country; and there were "extreme cases," he acknowledged, "where the universal resource is a dictator or martial law." [11] Nowhere in the Constitution are there any references to emergency executive power, but one provision does recognize the concept of a national emergency so extreme as to warrant some abridgment of personal liberty. That is the clause permitting the privilege of the writ of habeas corpus to be suspended "when in cases of rebellion or invasion the public safety may require it." If, however, the clause does furnish legitimation for the concept of national emergency, it also defines the phenomenon in exceedingly narrow terms—not war of any kind, but only a state of invasion; not domestic disorder of any kind, but only a state of rebellion. In fact, there have been only two such emergencies since the Constitution was written, and none after 1865.

Yet the greatest growth of emergency executive power has occurred during the twentieth century. Among the notable examples of its exercise are Franklin Roosevelt's order for the virtual imprisonment of some 112,000 Japanese-Americans in 1942, and Harry Truman's order for seizure of the nation's steel mills in 1952. That this concept of extraordinary action in response to desperate necessity has been normalized and even trivialized to the point of becoming a menace not only to the American public but to the presidency itself, seems amply demonstrated in the conduct and downfall of Richard Nixon.

It is a long way from the splendor of emancipation to the shame of Watergate, and yet a line of historical influence runs between them. Makers of the modern "imperial presidency" have drawn heavily on the example and immortal fame of Abraham Lincoln for vindication of their actions, conveniently ignoring the extent to which precedents taken from the Civil War are rendered invalid by its uniqueness. It is accordingly possible to conclude that Lincoln's use of executive power was wise and appropriate in its context, but not an unmixed blessing as a presidential tradition.

As Lincoln, after the attack on Fort Sumter, began to extend the grasp of executive authority, one of the questions arising was whether his course of action would be impeded in any serious degree by judicial intervention. The first answer came within a matter of six weeks from the chief justice of the United States. Roger B. Taney, now eighty-four years old, went out of his way to challenge the presidential policy of military arrest. At a time when the fate of Maryland seemed to hang in the balance and pro-Confederate rioting in Baltimore threatened to isolate Washington from the rest of the country, he issued a writ of habeas corpus for one John Merryman, a leading Maryland secessionist accused of sabotage and other treasonable activities. The commanding general refused to honor the writ on the grounds that the privilege had been suspended by presidential authority. Taney promptly ordered the general's arrest for contempt of court, but the federal marshal was barred from entering Fort McHenry to carry it out. Taney then acknowledged that he could do nothing more in Merryman's behalf. He nevertheless called upon the president to "perform his constitutional duty" by enforcing the judicial process. Within a week, he added a written opinion declaring that military arrest of civilians and presidential suspension of the writ of habeas corpus were both in violation of the Constitution.[12] Lincoln made no reply to Taney except indirectly by defending his policy in a message to Congress and by continuing to follow it as though the chief justice had never spoken.

Ex parte Merryman, says one scholar, "struck the first mighty blow in federal court history on behalf of individual liberties."[13] Yet it is unlikely that Taney had any greater love for personal freedom than did Lincoln, and as for the handling of public disorder, he once expressed the view that rioters should be fired upon when they cast their first stone.[14] He was actually less interested in protecting civil liberties than in defending the precincts of judicial power against military intrusion. But the biggest difference between the two men in 1861 came to this—the president thought that the Union was worth saving at almost any cost, whereas the chief justice did not think that it was worth saving at all. Taney's sympathies were with the Confederacy. He favored peaceable separation, considered the war a descent into madness, detested Republicans as a class, and regarded the Lincoln administration as a hateful despotism. By no recorded public or private utterance did he ever lend encouragement to the cause of the Union. It is testimony, perhaps, to the stability of the American constitutional system that he should have continued in office, without any serious threat of removal, until his death late in 1864.

"From the Civil War down to our own day," writes the constitutional scholar Bernard Schwartz, "the consensus of learned opinion has been that, on the legal issue involved in *Merryman*, Taney was right and Lincoln was wrong." [15] As early as 1866 in *Ex parte Milligan*, with Lincoln's friend David Davis delivering the opinion, the Supreme Court went part way toward saying the same thing. This merely signified, however, that with the war over, it was better for the public safety to repudiate much of what had so recently been considered vitally necessary. In the overwhelming "now" of 1861, Taney may have been just as wrong as Lincoln had become by 1866. Nearly a century later, Justice Robert H. Jackson still pondered the paradox: "Had Mr. Lincoln scrupulously observed the Taney policy," he said, "I do not know whether we would have had any liberty, and had the Chief Justice adopted Mr. Lincoln's philosophy as the philosophy of the law, I again do not know whether we would have had any liberty." [16]

Lincoln's cool disregard of the *Merryman* opinion has sometimes been taken as an indication of his attitude toward the judiciary in general, and also as exemplifying the sunken prestige of the Supreme Court during the Civil War era. Neither of these impressions is substantially accurate, but some advantage may accrue from examining each of them.

Republican denunciation of the *Merryman* opinion was all the more vehement, of course, because it had been written by the author of the *Dred Scott* decision. The odium of the *Dred Scott* case was attached primarily to individual justices, however. The extent to which it undermined the Supreme Court as an institution has been considerably exaggerated. Too much attention has been given to the noisy but unavailing demands of a few antislavery radicals for reorganization of the Court and severe restrictions on its power. Republicans might indulge in fervid oratory about not bowing down to this "judicial Vatican," but for the most part, they wanted to change only the membership of the Court, not its structure and functions.

There had been six justices forming the majority that declared the Missouri Compromise unconstitutional in the *Dred Scott* case. Only four of them continued to serve on the Court during the Civil War, and three of those four (including two Southerners) soon proved themselves to be strong Unionists. Taney alone remained unrepentant and unredeemed, as it were, and Taney alone was responsible for *Ex parte Merryman*, a proceedings at chambers with which the rest of the Court had nothing to do. The often venomous hostility of many radical Republicans followed the chief justice into his grave, but one should not make the mistake of assuming that it was directed at the Supreme Court as a whole.

After the war began, the Republicans virtually nullified the two main parts of the *Dred Scott* decision; for Congress abolished slavery in the territories, and Lincoln's attorney general ruled that free blacks were citizens. No such attack was launched against the Supreme Court, however. A reorganization act, passed at Lincoln's urging in 1862, was eminently moderate and designed primarily to bring the circuit court system into adjustment with recent population changes. The Court, although it had few opportunities to review wartime legislation and executive orders, generally upheld administration policies, or at least acquiesced in them. At one point, it refused on technical grounds to hear a case that presented issues similar to those in *Ex parte Merryman*. Furthermore, Lincoln's appointees to the Court made it increasingly respectable in Republican eyes, the climax coming when Salmon P. Chase succeeded Taney as chief justice in December 1864. On the whole, then, if one remembers that Taney was an exceptional case, and if one takes into account the fact that the Supreme Court has always tended to play a somewhat subdued role in wartime, it appears that the Civil War Court, far from suffering a decline in prestige, actually gained back some of the prestige sacrificed in the *Dred Scott* decision.

Lincoln is usually listed among presidential critics of the Supreme Court, along with Jefferson, Jackson, and Franklin Roosevelt, but the nature and limits of his criticism should be understood with some precision. The practice of law had been his career for a quarter of a century, and he had once said that reverence for the law should become "the *political religion* of the nation." There is accordingly no doubt of his great respect for the judicial process, but he did not believe that public policy should be made in the courtroom. It would be "much safer for all," he maintained, if bad laws were obeyed and swiftly repealed rather than being violated in the hope of having them declared unconstitutional.[17]

This does not mean that Lincoln condemned the institution of judicial review. He did, however, reject the doctrine of judicial supremacy. That is, he acknowledged the power of the Supreme Court to refuse enforcement of a statute on the grounds that it was contrary to the Constitution, but he denied that the rationale of such a decision instantaneously and automatically became constitutional law, binding even upon the legislative and executive branches of the federal government. Instead, the rationale of the decision must be legitimated over a period of time by judicial reiteration, legislative acquiescence, and public sanction. Thus, in 1858, Lincoln announced his refusal to obey the *Dred Scott* decision as a "political rule," adding more specifically: "If I were in Congress, and a vote should come up on a question whether slavery should be prohibited in a new territory, in spite of that Dred Scott decision, I would vote that it should." In his inaugural address three years later, with Taney sitting nearby, he declared that Supreme Court decisions were binding on the parties involved and were "also entitled to very high respect and consideration, in all parallel cases, by all other departments of the government." Then he added: "At the same time the candid citizen must confess that if the policy of the government, upon vital questions, affecting the whole people, is to be irrevocably fixed by decisions of the Supreme Court, the instant they are made, in ordinary litigation between parties . . . the people will have ceased, to be their own rulers, having, to that extent, practically resigned their government into the hands of that eminent tribunal."[18]

It scarcely need be said that this warning has gone unheeded in the twentieth century, when much control over public policy has been transferred from legislative bodies to courts of law. Plainly, whatever Lincoln may have contributed by influence and example to the growth of federal power and to the creation of the imperial presidency, he bears no responsibility for the modern triumph of judicial supremacy.

Running like a golden thread across the entire fabric of Lincoln's constitutional thought is the theme of government by the people. He insisted that the war for the Union was a crucial test of the viability of popular government, and more specifically, a test of "whether any government, not *too* strong for the liberties of its people, can be strong *enough* to maintain its own existence, in great emergencies."[19] At the same time, his Reconstruction program was inspired in considerable part by an excessive eagerness to restore self-government in the South. And he found the idea of judicial supremacy repugnant because judge-made law is paternalistic, rather than democratic; indeed, he took the extreme view that the ultimate power to interpret the Constitution rests with the people themselves, who authorized it and ratified it in the first place.

One of the paradoxes of freedom is that it means both sharing authority and exemption from authority. To Lincoln, the Constitution was essentially an arrangement for the sharing of authority—that is, a structure of self-government. In practice, this meant majority rule, limited by certain guarantees of individual rights, in a system of representative government. During ordinary times, the primary instrument of majoritarian representative democracy was the legislature, which could best reflect and respond to the diverse attitudes and interests of the people. Only an extreme emergency in which the single purpose of national self-preservation overrode all other considerations could justify his own assumption of extraordinary executive powers, and even then he remained responsible to the people. "Their will, constitutionally expressed," he declared, "is the ultimate law for all. If they should deliberately resolve to have immediate peace even at the loss of their country, and their liberty, I know not the power or the right to resist them. It is their own business, and they must do as they please with their own."[20]

Lincoln spoke these words shortly before the election of 1864, when it appeared that a war-weary nation might decide to write off the Union and three years of sacrifice by turning him out of office. Responding to talk of a coup d'etat and other wild rumors, he promised categorically that his opponent, if elected, would be duly installed as president on the day appointed by law. Thus he placed the principle of self-government above even his passion for the Union. More than that, he affirmed his adherence to the most critical and most fragile principle in the democratic process—namely, the requirement of minority submission to majority will.

This principle, Lincoln believed, was the one most clearly at stake in the war. "If the minority will not acquiesce," he said, "the majority must, or the government must cease. There is no other alternative; for continuing the government, is acquiescence on one side or the other." He rejected the argument that the people of the Confederacy were fighting for their own version of self-government. Southern independence had never in itself been the goal of more than a small minority. The purpose of secession, first as a threat and then as a reality, was the protection of slavery, an institution by nature incompatible with the ideal of self-government. It was the act of a coercive minority attempting to impose its will upon the majority, an act that had no sanction either in the Constitution or in the right of revolution. "If, by the mere force of numbers," he acknowledged in his first inaugural, "a majority should deprive a minority of any clearly written constitutional right, it might in a moral point of view, justify revolution. . . . But such is not our case. All the vital rights of minorities, and of individuals, are so plainly assured to them . . . in the Constitution, that controversies never arise concerning them."[21]

The complacency of this pronouncement on the state of civil liberties in his time suggests that Lincoln may have given more thought to the meaning of government *by* the people than to the implications of government *for* the people. His emphasis on majoritarian democracy as the institutional basis for personal freedom seems inadequate and almost irrelevant in our modern society, preoccupied to the verge of obsession with defining the rights of proliferating minorities. Majority rule, as embodied especially in legislative assemblies, appears more and more to constitute democratic inertia in a world of accelerating social change. It is the anvil on which powerful and sometimes coercive minorities hammer out decisions affecting the whole people.

Perhaps the time has come to remind ourselves that although there can be majority rule without minority rights, it is unlikely that minority rights could survive very long if majority rule were allowed to disintegrate. "The ultimate power of the majority," says Bertrand Russell "is very important to minimize the harshness inevitably involved in great changes, and to prevent a rapidity of transformation which causes a revulsion of feeling."[22] Here Russell has suggested a mediative theory of majority rule that may be more realistic than Lincoln's conception of majorities as the principal initiators of social action. The two dynamic elements in any effort at major social change are usually two intensely hostile minorities, one supporting the change and one resisting it. The function of the majority, however passive it may seem, is to restrain, delay, moderate, and finally absorb the dynamic force of change and then bring it to bear, gradually but insistently, on the dynamic force of resistance.

This was not Lincoln's model of majority rule. Yet there were times when he used Congress and the American public in precisely this way, as a massive mediative force between two hostile minorities, notably the Radical Republicans and the War Democrats, whose help he needed in the struggle for the Union. More than he intended or realized, Lincoln in his conduct of the presidency may have anticipated the future and incorporated it in the present.

NINE

Lincoln, the Civil War, and the American Mission

RICHARD N. CURRENT

The end of the Civil War was almost in sight when, on March 4, 1865, Abraham Lincoln delivered his second inaugural address. Looking back four years to the start of the conflict, he then said with reference to the Confederacy and the Union, Jefferson Davis and himself: "Both parties deprecated war; but one of them would *make* war rather than let the nation survive; and the other would *accept* war rather than let it perish. And the war came." [1]

Why had Lincoln been willing to take the risk of war? Why was he determined to save the Union even at the possible cost of horrendous bloodshed? Was there no other choice?

After Lincoln's election in November 1860, the nation faced a secession crisis with the anticipation of the first step by South Carolina, which took that step on December 20, leading the way for the withdrawal of the rest of the states of the lower South. Congress and the Northern people discussed three possible courses for the federal government to follow.

One was, in the words of Horace Greeley, the influential editor of the *New York Tribune*, to "let the erring sisters go in peace," that is, to let the seceding states leave, and good riddance to them (though, in fact, Greeley did not intend to let them go unless they met certain fairly strict conditions that he prescribed). The second proposal was to find some compromise that would hold the states together. After all, there had been threats of disunion before, and the danger had been averted each time—by the Missouri Compromise, the compromise tariff of 1833, and the Compromise of 1850. Why not a compromise of 1860 now? The third possibility was, in the phrase of its advocates, to "enforce the laws" of the federal government. Though to its friends a simple matter of law and order, this seemed to its opponents like the "coercion" of sovereign states. The use of force against the states was, in the eyes of many Southerners, an evil to be resisted by force.[2]

The third of these choices was Lincoln's first, the one he favored from the outset. He was not making a deliberate decision for war, however, when he decided to provision Fort Sumter, to reinforce it if provisioning should be resisted, and in either case to make at least a show of maintaining the federal authority. We need not turn aside even to consider the old Confederate charge, repeated by Southern historians as recently as a generation ago, that Lincoln consciously and cleverly "maneuvered" the Confederates into firing the first shot so as to provoke a war that would save him, his party, and his country. The fact is that Jefferson Davis and the Confederates had already made their decision to capture the fort, and they would very soon have attacked it even if Lincoln had never thought of sending an expedition there. So much for the provocation charge. But it is quite a different thing to suggest that Lincoln considered the possibility, indeed the probability, of a conflict of arms resulting from his provisioning attempt. And it is not too much to say—for he said it himself—that he was determined to manage the project in such a way as to put the blame for war, if war should ensue, clearly and unmistakably upon the other side.[3]

As for compromise, Lincoln had never given it serious consideration. He did not pursue the idea of removing the garrison from Fort Sumter in exchange for the adjournment of the Virginia secession convention, if indeed he ever really entertained the idea. He showed little enthusiasm for the work of the congressional committees on compromise, or for that of the Washington peace conference. True, he endorsed at least one of the constitutional amendments that Senator John J. Crittenden, of his own native Kentucky, proposed—the one to guarantee slavery forever in the states where it existed. But Lincoln rejected the key part of the Crittenden Compromise, that is, the proposal to run an East-West line through the territories and permit slavery below the line. To him, this plan was unacceptable on political grounds, the Republican platform having been built upon a free-soil plank, which called for the complete exclusion of slavery from the territories. The Crittenden plan, as he viewed it, was also wrong in principle and would be a failure in practice. To allow slavery south of a particular line would only be to invite proslavery expansionists to annex all the territory they could to the south of it—in the Caribbean and in Central America. Any plan, if it were to have a chance with the secessionists, would have to concede, at the very least, the right of slavery to expand. To Lincoln, therefore, compromise did not seem like a real alternative.[4]

Nor did the other possibility—to "let the erring sisters go in peace," to accept disunion and learn to live with it. "Physically speaking, we cannot separate," Lincoln explained in his first inaugural. "We cannot remove our respective sections from each other, nor build an impassable wall between them." Inconceivable to Lincoln in 1861 was anything, on this continent, like the Berlin Wall of 1961 or the long strip of minefield and barbed wire that keeps apart the two halves of divided Germany. "Suppose you go to war, you cannot fight always"; Lincoln went on, addressing the disaffected people of the South, "and when, after much loss on both sides, and no gain on either, you cease fighting, the identical old questions, as to terms of intercourse, are again upon you."[5] What Lincoln really wanted, of course, was continued union together with continued peace.

Yet he was ready, if it should come to that, to sacrifice peace for the Union. "The only thing like passion or infatuation in the man," Walt Whitman was later to say of him, "was the passion for the Union of These States."[6] Not that Lincoln was an unthinking superpatriot, a mere chauvinist. He was a nationalist, to be sure, but one of a special, unselfish, idealistic sort. "He loved his country partly because it was his own country, but mostly because it was a free country; and he burned with a zeal for its advancement, prosperity and glory, because he saw in such, the advancement, prosperity and glory, of human liberty, human right, and human nature."[7] That is a quotation from Lincoln's eulogy of Henry Clay, but the words fit Lincoln himself equally well, or better. He, too, saw the cause of all humanity in the cause of the Union. America the hope of the world!

This last conviction did not originate with either Clay or Lincoln. It had found expression much earlier, among statesmen and thinkers of the young Republic and even of the English colonies while they were new. Indeed, the idea goes back to the very discovery of America. It once applied to South America as well as North—to the whole of the Western Hemisphere. The New World was to be a model for the Old. Such was the belief in the beginning.

Christopher Columbus started the great American Dream, the vision of a land of innocence as well as abundance, a land that by its very existence was a rebuke to Europe. On returning from his first voyage of discovery, in 1493, Columbus wrote the sovereigns of Spain a letter in which he described the New World's inhabitants as a carefree people who wore no clothes, had no weapons, fought no wars, laid claim to no private property, but lived on terms of perfect equality and, without having to work, received from a bounteous nature everything they needed.

This picture, elaborated by other travelers, had a revolutionary effect on European thought. It provoked a crisis of conscience. If there was, somewhere, a continent with human beings who enjoyed equality, peace, and general happiness, then what curse must have fallen upon Europe to account for so much misery and strife! Sir Thomas More commented upon the ills of contemporary England through the Utopia that he located in the New World. Jean Jacques Rousseau hailed the natural man of America as an exemplar for the poor European, the victim of a corrupting civilization. The image of pristine America helped to prepare the way for reform and revolution in Europe—and in America as well.[8]

Unlike Rousseau, the Puritans of New England saw evil in the wilderness, yet they too looked upon the New World as the home, at least prospectively, of the ideal society. The building of such a society, as an example for all mankind, was the task to which they set themselves. With God's cooperation they hoped to succeed, but they had a feeling that, succeed or fail, they were being watched. "For we must consider that we shall be as a City upon a hill," John Winthrop advised his fellow colonists in a sermon he wrote on shipboard approaching Massachusetts Bay in 1630. "The eyes of all people are upon us. Soe that if we shall deal falsely with our God in this work we have undertaken, and so cause him to withdraw his present help from us, we shall be made a story and a by-word throughout the world."[9] Descendants of the Puritans were to identify God's chosen people with the citizens of the United States.

The United States came into being supposedly as a delayed fulfillment of God's and nature's promise. Obviously the promise of the New World had not been realized before 1776, not in the English colonies at any rate, for the colonists had much to complain about. The fault must be the continuing and corrupting influence of the mother country; the cure, a complete separation from it. In the Declaration of Independence Thomas Jefferson wrote confidently of "self-evident" truths—"that all men are created equal, that they are endowed by their Creator with certain unalienable Rights, that among these are Life, Liberty, and the pursuit of Happiness." These propositions were by no means self-evident before the discovery of America. In presenting them Jefferson was echoing John Locke, but, consciously or not, he was also catching the distant echo of Christopher Columbus.

Those who believed the revolutionary war was being fought for more than mere independence—and George Washington was one of them—did not feel that the Revolution ended with the war. General Washington doubtless expressed the aspirations of many when, in 1783, he sent a circular to the various states to announce the final victory and to urge the formation of a strong national government. He said:

> The Citizens of America, placed in the most enviable condition, as the sole lords and Proprietors of a vast Tract of Continent, comprehending all the various soils and climates of the World, and abounding with all the necessaries and conveniencies of life, are now by the late satisfactory pacification, acknowledged to be possessed of absolute freedom and independency, They are, from this period, to be considered as the Actors on a most conspicuous Theater, which seems to be peculiarly designated by Providence for the display of human greatness and felicity; Here, they are not only surrounded with every thing which can contribute to the completion of private and domestic enjoyment, but Heaven has crowned all its other blessings, by giving a fairer opportunity for political happiness, than any other Nation has ever been favored with. . . . The foundation of our Empire was not laid in the gloomy age of Ignorance and Superstition, but at an Epocha when the rights of mankind were better understood . . . than at any former period."

Washington went on to say that there was "an option still left to the United States of America." Its people could choose their own destiny. "This is the time of their political probation," he said in language reminiscent of Winthrop, "this is the moment when the eyes of the whole World are turned upon them, this is the moment to establish or ruin their national Character forever."

And in language anticipating Lincoln: "It is yet to be decided, whether the Revolution must ultimately be considered as a blessing or a curse: . . . not to the present age alone, for with our fate will the destiny of unborn Millions be involved."[10]

The Revolution found fulfillment in the Constitution of 1787. Here was another instance of God's favor to the United States and another example to the rest of the world. So it seemed to President Washington, among others. In his Farewell Address, 1796, he imparted to his fellow citizens his hope "that Heaven may continue to you the choicest tokens of its beneficence . . . that the free constitution . . . may be sacredly maintained . . . that, in fine, the happiness of the people of these States, under the auspices of liberty, may be made complete, by so careful a preservation and so prudent a use of this blessing as will acquire to them the glory of recommending it to the applause, the affection, and adoption of every nation which is yet a stranger to it."

In the same address the president advised the people to keep the New World politically apart from the Old. "Why, by interweaving our destiny with that of any part of Europe, entangle our peace and prosperity in the toils of European Ambition, Rivalship, Interest, Humor, or Caprice?" [11] Underlying the young Republic's policy of diplomatic independence was the persisting belief in the degeneracy and hopelessness of Europe, the vigor and potentiality of America.

There was, of course, a difference between the theory of American virtue and the fact of American vice, a difference that European critics never tired of pointing out. The imperfections of the United States—the persistence of slavery, the rise of an aggressive, expansionist spirit—became more and more visible during the first half of the nineteenth century. Believers in the American Dream had to take an increasingly apologetic stand. Daniel Webster, along with many others, was ashamed of his country's role in pursuit of what some called its Manifest Destiny. "I have always wished," he said in criticizing the annexation of Texas, "that this country should exhibit to the nations of the earth the example of a great, rich, and powerful republic, which is not possessed by a spirit of aggrandizement. It is an example, I think, due from us to the world, in favor of the character of republican government." [12] In opposing the Mexican War he repeated his wish that "this country should exhibit to the world the example of a powerful republic, without greediness and hunger of empire." To Webster it seemed that democracy—or republicanism—could be spread much more successfully by the force of example than by the force of arms.

Lincoln, as one of Webster's fellow Whigs, also spoke out against the war with Mexico. From the 1830s on he became more and more concerned about proslavery expansionism and proslavery lawlessness. After the mob killing of the Alton abolitionist Elijah Lovejoy he lectured to the young men of Springfield on the threat to the future of democracy. Lincoln and his contemporaries could hardly pretend that the democratic ideals of the Declaration of Independence had been brought even close to realization. But he was no less devoted to the ideals because of that. He came to look upon the United States as an experiment to see if the principles of the Declaration and the Constitution could be made to work. The experiment, he believed, was of vital interest not only to Americans but also to the whole "family of man," for the outcome would determine the future of self-government throughout the world.

Defenders of slavery began, in their desperateness, to repudiate the principles of the Declaration. In 1848 John C. Calhoun, the South Carolina nullificationist, denounced as "the most false and dangerous of all political errors" the proposition that "all men are born free and equal." Calhoun proceeded to aver: "Taking the proposition literally . . . there is not a word of truth in it. It begins with 'all men are born,' which is utterly untrue. Men are not born. Infants are born." [13] (Of course, the phrase in the Declaration actually reads "all men are *created*"; Calhoun's distortion of it shows how desperate he was for an argument.) He insisted that, if the Union should ever break up, the root cause of the catastrophe would be the propagation of the idea of human equality and freedom. (Here Calhoun was probably right.)

Lincoln deplored the propaganda of those who, as he put it, were "beginning to assail and to ridicule the white-man's charter of freedom—the declaration that 'all men are created free and equal.'" He commented: "This sounds strangely in republican America. The like was not heard in the fresher days of the Republic." [14] Americans, some of them, were falling away from the great secular faith of their fathers.

The "white-man's charter of freedom," Lincoln had called it. What about the black man? Was not he, too, created free and equal? Was not the Declaration also the black man's charter? More and more, Lincoln by his own logic was driven in the direction of an affirmative answer. In 1854 he said: "When the white man governs himself that is self-government; but when he governs himself, and also governs *another* man, that is *more* than self-government—that is despotism. If the Negro is a *man*, why then my ancient faith teaches me that 'all men are created equal;' and that there can be no moral right in connection with one man's making a slave of another." [15] At that time Lincoln left unspoken the next conclusion to be drawn from the same logic, namely, that there could be no moral right in one man's making a social and political inferior of another merely because of race.

In 1858, however, Lincoln expounded the Declaration in such a way as to carry his reasoning much further. "I think the authors of that notable instrument intended to include *all* men," he said in one of his debates with Stephen A. Douglas, "but they did not intend to declare all men equal *in all respects*. . . . They defined with tolerable distinctness, in what respects they did consider all men created equal—equal in 'certain inalienable rights, among which are life, liberty, and the pursuit of happiness.'" The authors of the Declaration were quite aware of the fact that, in 1776, blacks did not enjoy full equality with whites, and whites did not enjoy full equality with one another. The authors did not pretend to be describing American society as it actually existed at that time. Lincoln continued: "They meant to set up a standard maxim for free society, which should be familiar to all, and revered by all; constantly looked to, constantly labored for, and even though never perfectly attained, constantly approximated, and thereby constantly spreading and deepening its influence, and augmenting the happiness and value of life to all people of all colors everywhere." [16]

To "all people of all colors everywhere"! Lincoln still saw the American ideal as an inspiration for the rest of the world. But it could be an effective inspiration for others only to the extent that Americans lived up to it themselves. Lincoln said he hated Douglas's attitude of indifference toward the spread of slavery into new territories. "I hate it because of the monstrous injustice of slavery itself," he explained. "I hate it because it deprives our republican example of its just influence in the world—enables the enemies of free institutions, with plausibility, to taunt us as hypocrites." [17] Lincoln condemned the antiforeigner, anti-Catholic Know-Nothing movement for much the same reason. "As a nation," he wrote, "we began by declaring that '*all men are created equal*.' We now practically read it 'all men are created equal, *except Negroes*.' When the Know-Nothings get control, it will read 'all men are created equal, except Negroes, *and foreigners, and catholics*.' When it comes to this I should prefer emigrating to some country where they make no pretence of loving liberty—to Russia, for instance, where despotism can be taken pure, and without the base alloy of hypocrasy." [18]

When the secession crisis arose in 1860, Lincoln felt that the United States was on trial before the world—much as Winthrop, more than two centuries earlier, had thought the colony of Massachusetts Bay on trial. After the coming of the Civil War, Lincoln developed and perfected an idea he had expressed as early as 1838. Referring to our revolutionary forefathers, he then had said: "Their ambition aspired to display before an admiring world, a practical demonstration of the truth of a proposition, which had hitherto been considered, at best no better, than problematical, namely, *the capability of a people to govern themselves.*" In his July 4, 1861, message to Congress, his first message after the fall of Fort Sumter, he declared that the issue between North and South involved more than the future of the United States. "It presents to the whole family of man, the question, whether a Constitutional republic, or a democracy—a government of the people, by the same people—can, or cannot, maintain its territorial integrity, against its own domestic foes." And finally at Gettysburg he made the culminating, the supreme statement, concluding with the familiar words: "that from these honored dead we take increased devotion to that cause for which they gave the last full measure of devotion—that we here highly resolve that these dead shall not have died in vain—that this nation, under God, shall have a new birth of freedom—and that government of the people, by the people, for the people, shall not perish from the earth." [19]

That is what the Civil War was about, as Lincoln saw it. That is what was at stake, in 1860, in the threatened "destruction of our national fabric, with all its benefits, its memories, and its hopes," to quote again from the first inaugural address.[20] That is why Lincoln could not consent to a peaceful separation of the Union; why he could not agree to a compromise at the sacrifice of free soil; why he chose to make, at Fort Sumter, a symbolic Union-saving gesture that might lead, and did lead, to a Union-saving war.

At stake was a tradition that stretched back through the founding of the Republic to the discovery of America: from Abraham Lincoln to George Washington, Thomas Jefferson, John Winthrop, and on back to Christopher Columbus. It had become the secular religion of the American people. Some today might refer to it as the great American myth. Let those be cynical who will. There is something to be said for such a secular religion, even in our own time, especially in our own time. It would not be altogether bad if American leaders still believed and still acted on the belief that the United States had a special calling—not a Manifest Destiny to expand and to conquer—but a sacred mission to set an example for the rest of the world by living up to its own historic ideals.

Notes

In all quotations the editors have retained the original spelling, punctuation, and emphasis.

Chapter 1: The Search for Identity and Love in Young Lincoln

1. W[illiam] D[ean] Howells, *Life of Abraham Lincoln* (Springfield, Ill.: Abraham Lincoln Association, 1938), pp. 32–33. Minutes from the New Salem Debating Society no longer exist, but the Illinois State Historical Library does have the minutes from the debating society in Petersburg. Membership in the societies overlap and the range of topics discussed was quite similar. One can therefore infer the nature of the New Salem Debating Society with some confidence from these records.

2. Russell Godby told William Herndon in 1865 that he once hired Lincoln to do some farmwork but to his surprise found him sitting on a woodpile reading a book. Godby asked Lincoln what he was reading. "I'm not reading," he answered. "I'm studying." "Great God Almighty!" Godby exclaimed and walked on. See William H. Herndon, and Jesse Weik, *Herndon's Life of Lincoln*, Introduction and Notes by Paul M. Angle (Cleveland and New York: World Publishing Co., Forum Books, 1942), p. 92. One should note, however, the literary qual-

ity of Charles James Fox Clarke's letters to his mother and brother from the village in the 1830s. See Charles R. Clarke, "Sketch of Charles James Fox Clarke with Letters to His Mother," *Journal of the Illinois State Historical Society* 22 (January 1930):559–81. Jack Kelso quoted Shakespeare and Burns with or without encouragement and Mentor Graham was sufficiently educated to assist Lincoln when he needed to learn some mathematics quickly. Finally Dr. Allen, as mentioned above, was a graduate of Dartmouth.

3. The best source on New Salem and Lincoln's life there is Benjamin P. Thomas, *Lincoln's New Salem: Its History, Its Influence on Lincoln, Its Lincoln Legends, and the Story of Its Restoration*, new and rev. ed. (1834; Chicago and Lincoln's New Salem: Lincoln's New Salem Enterprises, Inc., 1973). Most of the New Salem legends originate in Herndon and Weik, *Herndon's Lincoln*. The Clarke letters are among the few pieces of documentary evidence that exist on the village. Thomas effectively utilizes other contemporary sources such as newspapers.

4. After 1831 Thomas Lincoln and his wife, Sarah, lived in Coles

County, Illinois, some seventy miles from Springfield.

5. Roy P. Basler et al., eds., *The Collected Works of Abraham Lincoln*, 9 vols. (New Brunswick, N.J.: Rutgers University Press, 1953–55), 2:96–97.

6. Thomas, *Lincoln's New Salem*, pp. 81–82.

7. Basler, *Collected Works*, 1:510.

8. "'I was out of work,' he [Lincoln] said to me once, 'and there being no danger of more fighting, I could do nothing better than enlist again.'" Herndon and Weik, *Herndon's Lincoln*, p. 82.

9. Basler, *Collected Works*, 4:65.

10. Ibid., 4:64.

11. Ibid., p. 65.

12. Ibid.

13. Thomas, *Lincoln's New Salem*, pp. 102–3.

14. Harry E. Pratt, *The Personal Finances of Abraham Lincoln* (Springfield, Ill.: Abraham Lincoln Association, 1943), p. 13.

15. Thomas, *Lincoln's New Salem*, pp. 111–12.

16. Basler, *Collected Works*, 4:65.

17. Thomas, *Lincoln's New Salem*, pp. 95–96.

18. Ibid., p. 98. Note also Howells, *Life of Lincoln*, pp. 32–33.

19. Thomas, *Lincoln's New Salem*, pp. 96–97.

20. Basler, *Collected Works*, 1:25.

21. Thomas, *Lincoln's New Salem*, p. 101.

22. Basler, *Collected Works*, 3:16.

23. Ibid., 4:65.

24. Ibid.

25. After Lincoln's death, Dummer told Herndon that "Lincoln used to come to our office—Stuart's and mine—in Springfield from New Salem and borrow law books." Herndon and Weik, *Herndon's Lincoln*, p. 145 n.

26. Paul Simon, *Lincoln's Preparation for Greatness: The Illinois Legislative Years* (Norman: University of Oklahoma Press, 1965), pp. 277–78.

27. Ibid., pp. 232–36.

28. Most of Erikson's writings deal with Identity. Note especially *Childhood and Society*, 2d ed. (1950; New York: W. W. Norton & Co., 1963); *Identity: Youth and Crisis* (New York: W. W. Norton & Co., 1968); *Insight and Responsibility* (New York: W. W. Norton & Co., 1964); and *Young Man Luther* (New York: W. W. Norton & Co., 1958).

29. Benjamin Thomas, *Abraham Lincoln: A Biography* (New York: Alfred A. Knopf, 1952), p. 56.

30. Basler, *Collected Works*, 1:78–79.

31. Ibid., pp. 94–95.

32. Ibid., p. 118.

33. Ibid., p. 119.

34. Justin G. Turner and Linda Levitt Turner, *Mary Todd Lincoln: Her Life and Letters* (New York: Alfred A. Knopf, 1972), p. 11.

35. Ibid., p. 21.

36. Basler, *Collected Works*, 1:78.

37. Herndon and Weik, *Herndon's Lincoln*, pp. 163–82.

38. Ruth Painter Randall, *The Courtship of Mr. Lincoln* (Boston: Little, Brown and Co., 1957). Note also Randall's earlier book, *Mary Lincoln: Biography of a Marriage* (Boston: Little, Brown and Co., 1953).

39. Randall, *Mary Lincoln*, pp. 47–51, 64, and 70–71; Randall, *The Courtship*, pp. 117–28.

40. Randall, *The Courtship*, p. 125.

41. Randall, *Mary Lincoln*, p. 64.

42. Except, perhaps, by the women he loved.

43. Edmund Wilson, *Patriotic Gore: Studies in the Literature of the American Civil War* (New York: Oxford University Press, 1962), pp. 118–19.

44. Herndon and Weik, *Herndon's Lincoln*, p. 304.
45. Ibid., p. 163.
46. Emanuel Hertz, *The Hidden Lincoln: From the Letters and Papers of William H. Herndon* (New York: Viking Press, Blue Ribbon Books, 1940), p. 68.
47. Ibid., p. 374.
48. Ibid., pp. 259–60.
49. Milton H. Shutes, *Lincoln's Emotional Life* (Philadelphia: Dorrance & Co., 1957), pp. 68–69.
50. Herndon reported to Weik on January 5, 1889, a story reported to Herndon by Speed concerning Lincoln's visit to a prostitute. It is a preposterous story, however, that has Lincoln undressed and in bed with the girl before he asks how much she charged. On learning the fee was five dollars and aware that he had only three dollars, Lincoln got up and dressed but offered her the three dollars for her trouble. "Mr. Lincoln," she replied, "you are the most conscientious man I ever saw." In Hertz, *Hidden Lincoln*, p. 233. Somehow, one senses a Lincoln joke that got lost in translation. My argument for Lincoln's virginity is implicit in the discussion below. That argument, furthermore, is based on authenticated sources rather than Herndon's suspicious legends.
51. Erikson, *Childhood and Society*, p. 263.
52. Ibid., p. 264.
53. Joshua Fry Speed, *Reminiscences of Abraham Lincoln and Notes of a Visit to California: Two Lectures* (Louisville, Ky.: John P. Morton and Co., 1884), pp. 16–17.
54. Joshua F. Speed, "Incidents in the Early Life of A. Lincoln," memorandum to William Herndon, n.d. [after 1865], Joshua Speed Manuscript, Illinois State Historical Library.
55. Hertz, *Hidden Lincoln*, pp. 65–66. This personal letter is consistent with Herndon's treatment in *Herndon's Lincoln*, pp. 150–51 and with Speed's memorandum to Herndon, n.d., quoted in fn. 53. All commentators who have worked with this evidence agree that Lincoln therefore slept with Speed from 1837 to late December, 1840. Note Randall, *The Courtship*, p. 122; and Gary Lee Williams, "James and Joshua Speed: Lincoln's Kentucky Friends" (Ph.D. diss., Duke University, 1971), pp. 15–29. I agree with this reconstruction of events. However, it should be noted that Herndon contradicted himself in two letters to Jesse Weik. In Herndon to Weik, Springfield, January 15, 1886 (Hertz, *Hidden Lincoln*, p. 134), Herndon wrote: "Lincoln came to this city in 1837, and Joshua F. Speed gratuitously took him into his room, gave him bed and house room, etc. William Butler was a man of some wealth for the time . . . he took Lincoln to his house, gave him a bed, sleeping room, and boarded him from 1837 to 1842, when Lincoln got married to Miss Todd." The next day Herndon wrote again to Weik: "I intended to say that, in the Butler note, Butler gratuitously, freely, and without charge boarded Lincoln from 1837 to 1842, when Lincoln got married." See Hertz, *Hidden Lincoln*, p. 134. In these letters to Weik, Herndon was of course contradicting his own dating elsewhere as well as all the other evidence. The explanation seems to me to be a) Herndon's concern in those two letters to Weik was with Butler, not the establish-

ment of accurate dates. It was long after the event and he probably was simply confused; and b) Lincoln probably did stay with Butler after January, 1841, that is, after he left Speed's store. In other words, Lincoln stayed from 1837 to December, 1840, with Speed and from sometime in early 1841 to November, 1842, with Butler. Herndon simply collapsed the two in his 1886 letters to Weik, even though elsewhere he correctly dated Lincoln's stay with Speed. The importance of this question will become obvious below.

56. Herndon and Weik, *Herndon's Lincoln*, pp. 150–51.

57. Randall, *The Courtship*, pp. 11–17.

58. Speed, *Reminiscences of Lincoln*, p. 23.

59. Ward Hill Lamon, *The Life of Abraham Lincoln: From His Birth to His Inauguration as President* (Boston: James R. Osgood and Co., 1872), p. 483.

60. Hertz, *Hidden Lincoln*, p. 159.

61. Basler, *Collected Works*, 1:269.

62. Herndon wrote that "on the love question alone Lincoln opened to Speed possibly the whole." Hertz, *Hidden Lincoln*, p. 159.

63. Randall, *The Courtship*, variously characterizes Speed as "the frequent lover," p. 42; as having a "pleasing personality," p. 12; as "apt to fall in love with practically every pretty girl he encountered," p. 12; as having a "handsome Byronic face," p. 12; and as "that Don Juan of Springfield, Joshua Speed," p. 43.

64. To call Speed "frequent lover" and a "Don Juan" confuses mild flirtations with sexually consummated relationships. All the evidence indicates the former. Note Mary Todd to Mercy Ann Levering, Springfield, December 15, 1840, in Turner and Turner, *Mary Todd Lincoln*, p. 20; Lincoln to Speed, January 3, 1842, in Basler, *Collected Works*, 1:266; and the two references to Sarah Rickard in Lincoln to Speed, February 3, 1842, in ibid., 1:268, and Lincoln to Speed, March 27, 1842, in ibid., 1:282. As I argue here, Speed seemed to have the same kind of sexual conflicts as Lincoln, which in part explains their friendship; see n. 65, below.

65. Speed Memorandum to Herndon, November 30, 1866, Herndon-Weik Collection, Library of Congress.

66. The evidence in this paper complements nicely the fascinating article by Carroll Smith-Rosenberg, "The Female World of Love and Ritual: Relations between Women in Nineteenth-Century America," *Signs: Journal of Women in Culture and Society* 1 (Autumn 1975):1–29.

67. Paton Yoder, *Taverns and Travelers: Inns of the Early Midwest* (Bloomington: Indiana University Press, 1969), pp. 146–47.

68. Henry Clay Whitney, *Life on the Circuit with Lincoln*, Introduction and Notes by Paul M. Angle (Caldwell, Idaho: Caxton Printers, 1940), p. 62–63.

69. Speed wrote Herndon on September 17, 1866: "I sold out to Hurst 1 Jany 1841. And came to Ky in the spring," Herndon-Weik Collection. Also note the weekly announcements in the *Sangamo Journal*, beginning January 8, 1841: "The co-partnership heretofore existing between Jas. Bell and Joshua F. Speed is this day dissolved by mutual consent . . . January 1, 1841." A separate announcement noted the formation of the partnership of Bell and Charles R. Hurst, as of January 1, 1841.

70. Mary Todd wrote to Mercy Ann Levering in June, 1841: "Mr. Speed, our former most constant guest has been in Kentucky for some weeks past, will be here next month, on a visit perhaps, as he has some idea of deserting Illinois, his mother is anxious he should superintend her affairs, he takes a friend's privilege, of occasionally favouring me with a letter, in his last he spoke of his great desire of once more inhabiting this region & of his possibility of soon returning—," Turner and Turner, *Mary Todd Lincoln*, p. 27.
71. Erikson, *Insight and Responsibility*, p. 70.
72. Hertz, *Hidden Lincoln*, p. 37.
73. Basler, *Collected Works*, 1:228–29; Speed, *Reminiscences of Lincoln*, p. 39. The length of the depression is also confirmed by Mary Todd in a letter to Mercy Ann Levering, June, 1841. See Turner and Turner, *Mary Todd Lincoln*, p. 27.
74. For example, Lincoln to Speed, March 27, 1842, in Basler, *Collected Works*, 1:282.
75. Simon, *Lincoln's Preparation*, p. 239.
76. See Lincoln's thank-you note to Speed's half sister Mary, in Basler, *Collected Works*, 1:259–61.
77. Ibid., p. 261.
78. See above, n. 65; also Lincoln's letters to Speed, January 3, 1842; February 3, 1842; February 13, 1842; and February 25, 1842: Basler, *Collected Works*, 1:266.
79. Ibid.
80. Ibid., p. 269.
81. Ibid., p. 266.
82. Ibid., p. 267.
83. Ibid., p. 268.
84. Ibid., p. 280.
85. Ibid., p. 303. Lincoln also contemplated naming his first son after Speed; see p. 319.

Chapter 2:
Victorian Women and Domestic Life: Mary Todd Lincoln, Elizabeth Cady Stanton, and Harriet Beecher Stowe

1. Daniel Walker Howe, "American Victorianism as a Culture," *American Quarterly* 27 (December 1975): 507–32.
2. The Neolithic Revolution, or the transition in the Near East from food gathering to food production, began after 9000 B.C. and was completed by 5500 B.C., when "farming and stock breeding were well established and the basic level of the effective village farming community had been achieved" (Carlo M. Cipolla, *The Economic History of World Population*, 6th ed. [Baltimore: Penguin Books, 1974] p. 19). Nineteenth-century family planning was a part of the second revolution in human population—the Demographic Transition, or the transition from relatively high birth and death rates to relatively low birth and death rates. Ansley J. Coale, "The History of the Human Population," *The Human Population* (New York: Scientific American Book, 1974), pp. 15–28.
3. Edmund Wilson, *Patriotic Gore: Studies in the Literature of the American Civil War* (New York: Oxford University Press, 1962), pp. 25–35. I am grateful to Louis Dabney for reminding me of these printed letters.
4. Annie Fields, ed., *Life and Letters of Harriet Beecher Stowe* (Cambridge, Mass.: Riverside Press; Boston, New York: Houghton Mifflin and Co., 1897), p. 110; Wilson, *Patriotic Gore*, p. 17 [June 16, 1845].
5. Calvin Stowe to Harriet Beecher Stowe, September 30, 1844,

Beecher-Stowe Collection, Schlesinger Library on the History of Women in America, Cambridge, Mass., folder 61.

6. Fields, *Life and Letters*, p. 110 [June 16, 1845].

7. Wilson, *Patriotic Gore*, pp. 28–29 [July 29, 1855]. Summer correspondence between Harriet and Calvin Stowe continued for more than a decade to discuss the issues initially raised in 1844.

8. Fields, *Life and Letters*, p. 110 [June 16, 1845].

9. Calvin Stowe to Harriet Beecher Stowe, September 30, 1844, Beecher-Stowe Collection, folder 61.

10. Calvin Stowe to Harriet Beecher Stowe, June 30, 1844, Beecher-Stowe Collection, folder 61.

11. Catharine Beecher to Mary Beecher Perkins, Fall 1837, Beecher-Stowe Collection, folder 17.

12. Harriet Beecher Stowe to Calvin Stowe, July 19, 1844, Beecher-Stowe Collection, folder 69.

13. Charles Edward Stowe, *Life of Harriet Beecher Stowe: Compiled from Her Letters and Journals* (Boston: Houghton, Mifflin & Co., 1889), p. 115. I am grateful to Rebecca Veach for pointing out this letter to me. Daniel Scott Smith, "Family Limitation, Sexual Control, and Domestic Feminism in Victorian America," *Feminist Studies* 1, nos. 3–4 (Winter–Spring 1973), discusses the extent to which family limitation fostered a new kind of personal autonomy among Victorian women.

14. Alma Lutz, "Elizabeth Cady Stanton," in Edward T. James et al., eds., *Notable American Women, 1607–1950: A Biographical Dictionary*, 3 vols. (Cambridge, Mass.: Harvard University Press, Belknap Press, 1971), 3:342–47.

15. Wilson H. Grabill, Clyde V. Kiser, and Pascal K. Whelpton, "A Long View," in Michael Gordon, ed., *The American Family in Social-Historical Perspective* (New York: St. Martin's Press, 1973), pp. 374–95, esp. 387.

16. Robert V. Wells, "Family History and Demographic Transition," *Journal of Social History* 9 (Fall 1975): 6.

17. Harriet Beecher Stowe to Mary Dutton, December 13, 1838, Mary Dutton-Beecher Letters, Bienecke Library, Yale University.

18. Elizabeth Cady Stanton, *Eighty Years and More, Remininiscences 1815–1897* (1898; reprint ed., New York: Shocken, 1971), p. 114.

19. Catharine Beecher, *A Treatise on Domestic Economy: For the Use of Young Ladies at Home and at School*, rev. ed. (Boston: Thomas H. Webb & Co., 1843), p. 160. See also Kathryn Kish Sklar, *Catharine Beecher: A Study in American Domesticity* (New Haven: Yale University Press, 1973), pp. 151–68.

20. Beecher, *A Treatise*, pp. 36–37.

21. Ibid., p. 52.

22. See chap. 3, "Lincoln, Blacks, and Women."

23. Stanton, *Eighty Years*, p. 148.

24. Aileen Kraditor, ed., *Up from the Pedestal: Selected Writings in the History of American Feminism* (New York: Quadrangle Books, 1968), Introduction, p. 8.

25. This discussion of Mary Todd Lincoln relies on Justin G. Turner and Linda Levitt Turner, *Mary Todd Lincoln: Her Life and Letters* (New York: Alfred A. Knopf, 1972).

26. Ibid., p. 66.

27. Ibid., p. 41.

28. Ibid.

29. Willard King, *Lincoln's Manager, David Davis* (Cambridge,

Mass.: Harvard University Press, 1960), p. 84. I am extremely grateful to Rebecca Veach for bringing this letter to my attention. One alternate reading of Mary Lincoln's unusually prolonged nursing could be that she intended such nursing to act as a contraceptive method. In light of her rapid conception after Eddie's death, however, such a contraceptive motivation seems unlikely in Mary Lincoln at this time.

30. Turner and Turner, *Mary Todd Lincoln*, p. 237 and n., pp. 224–25, p. 355 and n.

31. Ibid., p. 21.

32. Ibid., p. 52.

33. Ibid., p. 534.

34. For a high critical estimate of Harriet Beecher Stowe's post-1857 fiction, see Alice Crozier, *The Novels of Harriet Beecher Stowe* (New York: Oxford University Press, 1969), pp. 85–151, and Henry F. May's "Introduction" to the John Harvard edition of *Oldtown Folks* (Cambridge, Mass.: Harvard University Press, 1966).

35. Turner and Turner, *Mary Todd Lincoln*, p. 128.

36. Stanton, *Eighty Years*, pp. 164, 166.

37. Barbara Welter, "The Cult of True Womanhood, 1820–1860," *American Quarterly* 28 (Summer 1966): 151–74.

38. Carroll Smith-Rosenberg, "Beauty, the Beast and the Militant Woman: A Case Study in Sex Roles and Social Stress in Jacksonian America," *American Quarterly* 23 (1971): 562–84; Nancy F. Cott, *The Bonds of Womanhood: New England Women 1780–1820* (New Haven: Yale University Press, 1976).

39. Smith-Rosenberg, "Beauty, the Beast, and the Militant Woman."

40. Ellen Carol DuBois, *Feminism and Suffrage, the Emergence of an Independent Women's Movement in America, 1848–1869* (Ithaca, N.Y.: Cornell University Press, 1978), p. 202.

Chapter 3:
Lincoln, Blacks, and Women

1. Roy P. Basler et al., eds., *The Collected Works of Abraham Lincoln*, 9 vols. (New Brunswick, N.J.: Rutgers University Press, 1953–55), 3:376.

2. Mary Boykin Chesnut, *A Diary from Dixie*, ed. Ben Ames Williams (Boston: Houghton Mifflin Co., 1949), p. 486.

3. Ibid., p. 382.

4. Ibid., p. 489.

5. Charles Francis Adams, *Familiar Letters of John Adams and His Wife Abigail Adams, during the Revolution, with a Memoir of Mrs. Adams* (New York: Hurd and Houghton, 1875), pp. 149–50.

6. Ibid., p. 155.

7. Ibid., p. 169.

8. Benjamin Quarles, *Frederick Douglass* (Washington, D.C.: Associated Publishers, 1948), p. 122.

9. Basler, *Collected Works*, 1:75.

10. Ibid., 2:501.

11. Ibid., 1:48.

12. Ibid., p. 94.

13. Ibid., p. 115.

14. Ruth Painter Randall, *Mary Lincoln: Biography of a Marriage* (Boston: Little, Brown and Co., 1953), p. 356.

15. Roy P. Basler, "And for His Widow and His Orphan," *Quarterly Journal of the Library of Congress* 27 (October 1970): 291–94.

16. Roy P. Basler, ed., *The Collected Works of Abraham Lincoln: Supplement, 1832–1865*, Contributions in American Studies, no. 7

(Westport, Conn., and London: Greenwood Press, 1974), p. 243.

17. Carl Sandburg, *Abraham Lincoln: The War Years*, 4 vols. (New York: Harcourt, Brace & Co., 1939), 2:573, 575; 4:117.

18. Sydney Greenbie and Marjorie Barstow Greenbie, *Anna Ella Carroll and Abraham Lincoln: A Biography* (Manchester, Maine: University of Tampa Press in co-operation with Falmouth Publishing Co., 1952), p. 353.

19. Basler, *Collected Works*, 5:381–82. This gives not only Lincoln's letter but in a footnote excerpts from Bates's letter and Miss Carroll's long letter dated August 14, 1862. The most complete account, including the text of Anna's letter is given in Greenbie and Greenbie, *Anna Ella Carroll*, pp. 351 ff.

20. Basler, *Collected Works*, 4:428 ff.

21. Avery Craven, *New York Herald Tribune Book Review*, October 26, 1952, p. 25.

22. Sandburg, *War Years*, 1:344.

23. Elizabeth Keckley, *Behind the Scenes: or, Thirty Years a Slave, and Four Years in the White House* (New York: G. W. Carleton & Co., 1868).

24. Basler, *Collected Works*, 6:365.

25. *New York Herald*, February 20, 1861.

26. Roy P. Basler, "Did President Lincoln Give the Smallpox to William Johnson," *Huntington Library Quarterly* 35 (May 1972): 279–84.

27. Quarles, *Frederick Douglass*, pp. 211–12. This book is the best scholarly treatment, and on it I have relied exclusively except where otherwise noted.

28. John Hay's diary gives the earlier date; Joseph T. Mills's diary the latter.

29. Frederick Douglass papers, Library of Congress.

30. Basler, *Collected Works*, 7:508.

31. Quarles, *Frederick Douglass*, pp. 218, 220.

32. Philip S. Foner, ed., *The Life and Writings of Frederick Douglass*, vol. 4, *Reconstruction and After* (New York: International Publishers, 1955), pp. 312, 313, 317.

33. Allen T. Rice, ed., *Reminiscences of Abraham Lincoln by Distinguished Men of His Time* (New York: North American Publishing Co., 1886), p. 193.

Chapter 4:
The Right to Rise

This essay touches on some of the highlights of my forthcoming *Lincoln and the Economics of the American Dream*. Because of the massiveness of the available evidence, the notes for the essay can be complete only for direct quotations. The other materials cited in the notes, in most cases, illustrate, rather than document, the questions under discussions.

1. Matthew Simpson, *Funeral Address Delivered at the Burial of President Lincoln, at Springfield, Illinois, May 4, 1865* (New York: Carlton & Porter, 1865), p. 17; Roy P. Basler et al., eds., *The Collected Works of Abraham Lincoln*, 9 vols. (New Brunswick, N.J.: Rutgers University Press, 1953–55), 1:178.

2. To illustrate, I was able to identify only twenty-four Lincoln speeches during the election year of 1840, although he probably made twice that number, if not more. The text of only one speech survives. (This focused on the advantage of national banking over other forms of monetary organization. So did Lincoln's other speeches—and his entire campaign. Cf. Albert J. Beveridge, *Abraham Lincoln, 1809–1858*, 2 vols. [Boston and

New York: Houghton Mifflin Co.; Cambridge, Mass.: Riverside Press, 1928], 1:263.) If we multiply the length of the extant speeches by twenty-four—and it would not be unreasonable to multiply by forty-eight or more —then Lincoln's speeches on banking, in a single year alone, had they been recorded, could have taken up a volume of his *Collected Works*. We should note, however, that the absence of good press coverage may have permitted Lincoln to repeat himself more routinely than he could do during the last few years of his life.

3. James Quey Howard's interview with George Close [May 1860], Abraham Lincoln Papers, Library of Congress; W[illiam] D[ean] Howells, *Life of Abraham Lincoln* (Springfield, Ill.: Abraham Lincoln Association, 1938), p. 28; Basler, *Collected Works*, 1:5–9, 61–69, 159–79; Paul Simon, *Lincoln's Preparation for Greatness: The Illinois Legislative Years* (1965; reprint ed., Urbana: University of Illinois Press, 1971), p. 212; Earl Schenck Miers, William E. Baringer and C. Percy Powell, eds., *Lincoln Day by Day: A Chronology, 1809–1865*, 3 vols. (Washington, D.C.: Lincoln Sesquicentennial Commission, 1960), 1:291.

4. *Illinois State Register*, December 12, 1840; *Journal of the Illinois House of Representatives*, 1840–41, pp. 79–80; *Laws of Illinois*, 1840–41, pp. 40–42. See also George William Dowrie, *The Development of Banking in Illinois, 1817–1863*, University of Illinois Studies in the Social Sciences 2, no. 4 (December 1913) (Urbana: University of Illinois, 1913), pp. 96–102; Bray Hammond, *Banks and Politics in America: From the Revolution to the Civil War* (Princeton, N.J.: Princeton University Press, 1957), p. 612.

5. Basler, *Collected Works*, 1:69.

6. Ibid., pp. 147–48; 2:15–17.

7. These expressions first appeared, respectively, in ibid., 2:4 and 1:69.

8. Ibid., 1:7–8; 5:282–83, 420, 522–23; 6:60–62; "Stephen T. Logan Talks about Lincoln," *Abraham Lincoln Association Bulletin* 12, September 1, 1928, p. 2; *Illinois State Journal*, November 5, 1864; William P. Fessenden to Thomas S. Pike, Roger Taney Papers, Library of Congress; Tyler Dennett, ed., *Lincoln and the Civil War in the Diaries and Letters of John Hay* (New York: Dodd, Mead, & Co., 1939), pp. 144–45; William O. Stoddard, *Inside the White House in War Times* (New York: C. L. Webster & Co., 1890), pp. 144–45 et passim.

9. Basler, *Collected Works*, 1:5–9, 136; *Journal of the Illinois House of Representatives*, 1834–35, pp. 69, 449–50.

10. Basler, *Collected Works*, 1:414, 407–16. Cf. H[enry] C. Carey, *Principles of Social Science*, 3 vols. (Philadelphia: J. B. Lippincott & Co., 1858); John Stuart Mill, *Principles of Political Economy* (London: Longmans, Green, Longmans, Albert & Green, 1865), pp. 566–67; William H. Herndon to Jesse K. Weik, January 1, 1886, Herndon-Weik Papers, Library of Congress.

11. Basler, *Collected Works*, 1:398–405; Samuel P. Ruggles to Edwin D. Morgan, November 28, 1862, Ruggles Letters, Illinois State Historical Library; *Fincher's Trades Review*, March 12, 1864.

12. Basler, *Collected Works*, 1:311; 3:357–58. On the inward-

oriented Whig mind, see especially Major L. Wilson, *Space, Time and Freedom: The Quest for Nationality and the Irrepressible Conflict, 1815–1861*, Contributions in American History, no. 35 (Westport, Conn.: Greenwood Press, 1974).

13. Basler, *Collected Works*, 1:132–34, 163–64.

14. The reconstruction of this episode by Ninian W. Edwards, Lincoln's brother-in-law, for Herndon is probably substantially accurate. William H. Herndon and Jesse W. Weik, *Herndon's Life of Lincoln*, Introduction and Notes by Paul M. Angle (Cleveland and New York: World Publishing Co., Forum Books, 1942), p. 157; cf. Basler, *Collected Works*, 1:320.

15. Dennett, *Diaries of Hay*, p. 143.

16. Eric Foner, *Free Soil, Free Labor, Free Men: The Ideology of the Republican Party before the Civil War* (New York: Oxford University Press, 1970), pp. 168–76.

17. Basler, *Collected Works*, 2:385 (4:168–69). See also A. Whitney Griswold, "The American Gospel of Success" (Ph.D. diss., Yale University, 1933), pp. 27, 35; Merrill D. Peterson, *The Jeffersonian Image in the American Mind* (New York: Oxford University Press, 1960), p. 221; Yehoshua Arieli, *Individualism and Nationalism in American Ideology* (1964; reprint ed., Baltimore: Penguin Books, 1966), pp. 308, 315, 318; John G. Cawelti, *Apostles of the Self-Made Man: Changing Concepts of Success in America* (Chicago: University of Chicago Press, 1965), pp. 42–43.

18. Basler, *Collected Works*, 4:169; Richard Hofstadter, *The American Political Tradition and the Men Who Made It* (New York: Alfred A. Knopf, 1948), p. 105.

19. Basler, *Collected Works*, 4:24–25. The viewpoint of this essay is presented without many misgivings in part because of the comforting knowledge that the raw material of the essay will permit able students, relying on diverse ideological perspectives, to see Lincoln in diverse ways. To illustrate, he might be portrayed as the politician and ideologist of the birthing industrial capitalist class readying for the climb to power in America—but still upholding its democratic and humanitarian illusions. Lincoln's persuasion thus can become, to borrow the phrase of Marx, another "*das Opium des Volk.*"

20. Basler, *Collected Works*, 5:487, 535; 6:24, 30, 362, 387–88; 7:145, 146–47, 185, 212, 217; 8:306, 317; Dennett, *Diaries of Hay*, p. 125; John Eaton, *Grant, Lincoln and the Freedmen: Reminiscences of the Civil War . . .* (New York: Longmans, Green, & Co., 1907), p. 168; Henry Samuels, "My Interview with Lincoln," Samuels MS, Illinois State Historical Library; G. S. Boritt, "The Voyage to the Colony of Linconia: The Sixteenth President, Black Colonization, and the Defense Mechanism of Avoidance," *Historian* 37 (1975): 619–37. The subject of Lincoln and Reconstruction still awaits a careful, modern monographer.

21. Often misunderstood as advancing the concept of a Union decreed by Nature, in fact Lincoln thought and spoke in terms of a nature harnessed by "steam, telegraph," in short man's economic might and intelligence. Basler, *Collected Works*, 4:259, 269; 5:53, 527–29.

22. The quote comes from Kenneth M. Stampp, *The Era of Reconstruction, 1865–1877* (New York:

Random House, Vintage Books, 1965), p. 42.

23. See, above all, Colin R. Ballard, *The Military Genius of Abraham Lincoln: An Essay* (1926; reprint ed., Cleveland: World Publishing Co., 1965); and T. Harry Williams, *Lincoln and His Generals* (New York: Random House, Vintage Books, 1952).

24. Basler, *Collected Works*, 8:150; cf. 1:135–36.

25. Ibid., 4:233.

26. Francis Lieber to Charles Sumner, August 31, 1864, Francis Lieber Papers, Huntington Library.

27. Basler, *Collected Works*, 4:235–36, 240. The italics in the Trenton speech are mine.

28. Ida M. Tarbell, *The Life of Abraham Lincoln*, 2 vols. (New York: Doubleday & McClure Co., 1900), 1:17 (cf. Benjamin P. Thomas, *Abraham Lincoln, A Biography* [New York: Alfred A. Knopf, 1952], pp. 3–4; Basler, *Collected Works*, 4:70); Clay in Allen Thorndike Rice, ed., *Reminiscences of Abraham Lincoln by Distinguished Men of His Time* (New York: North American Publishing Co., 1886), p. 297.

29. Basler, *Collected Works*, 4:240.

30. Ibid., 8:332–33.

Chapter 5:
The Apostle of Progress

1. Roy P. Basler et al., eds., *The Collected Works of Abraham Lincoln*, 9 vols. (New Brunswick, N.J.: Rutgers University Press, 1953–55), 3:463.

2. Ibid., 4:192.

3. See John G. Nicolay and John Hay, *Abraham Lincoln: A History*, 10 vols. (New York: Century Co., 1886), 1:44–46.

4. Ibid., pp. 85–86.

5. Ibid., p. 51.

6. Basler, *Collected Works*, 1:5.

7. Ibid., p. 6.

8. Ibid., pp. 24, 26.

9. Ibid., pp.29, 35, 39, 42.

10. Ibid., p. 40.

11. Ibid., pp. 69, 70.

12. Ibid., pp. 93, 182.

13. Nicolay and Hay, *Abraham Lincoln*, 1:129; Basler, *Collected Works*, 1:48, 78.

14. Nicolay and Hay, *Abraham Lincoln*, 1:134.

15. Basler, *Collected Works*, 1:54.

16. Nicolay and Hay, *Abraham Lincoln*, 1:135–36. For a complete discussion of the Illinois Internal Improvements project see Theodore C. Pease, *The Frontier State, 1818–1848*, Illinois Centennial Commission Series (Springfield, Ill.: 1918), p. 206–19. For one railroad in the system, see H. J. Stratton, "The Northern Cross Railroad," *Journal of the Illinois State Historical Society* 28 (July 1935): 5–52.

17. Nicolay and Hay, *Abraham Lincoln*, 1:137. For the progress of construction see the Vandalia *Free Press* as quoted in the Toledo *Blade*, December 27, 1837.

18. Nicolay and Hay, *Abraham Lincoln*, 1:158–59.

19. Basler, *Collected Works*, 1:122–23.

20. Ibid., pp. 135–37.

21. Ibid., p. 184.

22. Ibid., p. 196.

23. Ibid., pp. 243–44.

24. Ibid., pp. 250–51, 233.

25. Ibid., pp. 395–98.

26. Ibid., pp. 398–405.

27. Ibid., pp. 480–83.

28. Ibid., p. 484.

29. Ibid., p. 490.

30. Ibid., 2:98, 133, 211–12, 212–16.

31. Ibid., p. 325. For Lincoln's relations with the Illinois Central see Carlton J. Corliss, *Main Line of Mid-America: The Story of the Illinois Central* (New York: Crea-

tive Age Press, 1950), pp. 104–9.
32. Basler, *Collected Works*, 2:413–14, 415–22.
33. Ibid., p. 421.
34. Quoted in Corliss, *Main Line*, p. 86.
35. Basler, *Collected Works*, 3:462, 468.
36. Ibid., p. 472.
37. Ibid., p. 481.
38. Ibid., pp. 481, 482.
39. Ibid., 4:190.

Chapter 6:
The Search for Order and
Community

1. Henry V. Jaffa, *The Crisis of the House Divided: An Interpretation of the Issues in the Lincoln-Douglas Debates* (Garden City, N.Y.: Doubleday & Co., 1959); William J. Wolf, *The Religion of Abraham Lincoln*, rev. ed. (New York: Seabury Press, 1963); Edmund Wilson, *Patriotic Gore: Studies in the Literature of the American Civil War* (New York: Oxford University Press, 1962), pp. 99–130.
2. John William Ward, *Andrew Jackson: Symbol for an Age* (New York: Oxford University Press, 1955), pp. 49–50.
3. Ibid., pp. 51–53.
4. David Grimsted, "Rioting in Its Jacksonian Setting," *American Historical Review* 77 (April 1972): 367–68.
5. Ibid., p. 374.
6. Quoted in ibid., pp. 364–65.
7. This understanding of the division among American "conservatives" and the interpretation of the two positions presented below draw heavily on Perry Miller's *The Life of the Mind in America: From the Revolution to the Civil War* (New York: Harcourt, Brace & World, 1965).

8. Quoted in Miller, *Life of the Mind*, pp. 71–72.
9. Robert Baird, *Religion in America* (New York: Harper & Brothers, 1856), pp. 664–65.
10. The classic account of the evangelical sources of abolitionism is Gilbert Hobbs Barnes, *The Antislavery Impulse, 1830–1844* (New York: American Historical Association, D. Appleton-Century Co., 1933). See also Bertram Wyatt-Brown, *Lewis Tappan and the Evangelical War Against Slavery* (Cleveland: Press of Case Western Reserve University, 1969).
11. Quoted in Miller, *Life of the Mind*, p. 191.
12. Ibid., pp. 192–201, 147–50.
13. Ibid., pp. 208–9.
14. Ibid., pp. 149–55; for evidence of the persistence of the natural law tradition in legal thought see Robert Cover, *Justice Accused: Antislavery and the Judicial Process* (New Haven and London: Yale University Press, 1975).
15. Cover, *Justice Accused*, pp. 107–8, 243–49, and passim.
16. Roy P. Basler et al., eds., *The Collected Works of Abraham Lincoln*, 9 vols. (New Brunswick, N.J.: Rutgers University Press, 1953–55), 1:65, 69.
17. Ibid., 1:108–9.
18. Ibid., p. 112.
19. Ibid., pp. 113–14.
20. Ibid., pp. 114–15.
21. See Wilson, *Patriotic Gore*, pp. 106–8; and Jaffa, *A House Divided*, pp. 211–25.
22. This is not to say that there were no special twists—most notably with the seeming prophetic association of "towering genius" with radical action in regard to slavery. But it should be recalled that Lincoln did not rise to power because he proposed

emancipating slaves. He merely opposed the extension of slavery, partly because of his fear that it could lead to "enslaving free-men." Within his own frame of reference of the 1850s, the prophecy of the ambitious genius who would seek power "whether at the expense of emancipating slaves or enslaving freemen" could have been applied more properly to Douglas —with his amoral and dema-gogic indifference as to whether slavery was "voted up or down" —than to himself.

23. Basler, *Collected Works*, 1:272–73.
24. Ibid., 3:404.
25. Ibid., pp. 522–50.
26. Ibid., 4:200.
27. Philip S. Paludan, "The American Civil War Considered as a Crisis in Law and Order," *American Historical Review* 77 (October 1972): 1013–34.
28. Basler, *Collected Works*, 2:320.
29. See Don E. Fehrenbacher, *Prelude to Greatness: Lincoln in the 1850's* (Stanford, Calif.: Stanford University Press, 1962), chaps. 4, 5.
30. Basler, *Collected Works*, 3:550.
31. Ibid., 4:207.
32. Ibid., p. 270.
33. Ibid., 5:537.

Chapter 7:
Lincoln, Douglas, and Springfield in the 1858 Campaign

1. The population was figured on the basis of one voter to nine persons. The *Illinois State Journal* (hereafter, *Journal*) of January 28, 1858, estimated the Springfield population at 12,000. After the municipal election in April, the *Journal* of April 8 raised its guess to nearly 13,000.

2. Stephen A. Douglas to Charles H. Lanphier and George Walker, December 6, 1857, Charles H. Lanphier Papers, Illinois State Historical Library; published in Robert W. Johannsen, ed., *The Letters of Stephen A. Douglas* (Urbana: University of Illinois Press, 1961), p. 405. The Lanphier Papers have been photo-copied in a limited edition in Charles C. Patton, comp., *Glory to God and the Sucker Democracy: A Manuscript Collection of the Letters of Charles H. Lanphier*, 5 vols. (United States of America [Springfield, Ill.]: Frye-Williamson Press, privately printed, 1973).

3. Roy P. Basler et al., eds., *The Collected Works of Abraham Lincoln*, 9 vols. (New Brunswick, N.J.: Rutgers University Press, 1953–55), 2:240–47.

4. J. S. Roberts to Stephen A. Douglas, January 7, 1858, Stephen A. Douglas Papers, Regenstein Library, University of Chicago, Box 7, folder 20.

5. Thomas L. Harris to Lanphier, January 30, 1858, Lanphier Papers; Patton, *Glory to God*, vol. 4. Harris, from Petersburg, had re-placed Lincoln in Congress. Douglas's confidence in him was of long standing. In a detailed letter of strategy to Lanphier on December 18, 1854, giving directions on how to handle the U.S. Senate election in the legislature to secure the selection of James Shields and defeat Lincoln, Douglas advised Lanphier to show his letter only to Harris. "I have no secrets from him. I have implicit confidence in his discretion, firmness & fidelity. Tell him that he must take per-sonal charge of everything, and in no event leave Springfield even for a day during the Ses-

sion" (Lanphier Papers; Patton, *Glory to God*; vol. 2).

6. *Illinois State Register* (hereafter, *Register*), February 10, 1858.

7. *Journal*, January 30, 1858.

8. Ibid., February 19, 1858.

9. James A. Barret, who would be named one of the Douglas nominees for the legislature from Sangamon County, reported to Douglas on the simultaneous conventions of the two Democratic groups and on the Republicans' role in building up the Buchananites. Speaking of the Douglasites' convention, Barret declared that "Harmony and good feeling characterized its every proceeding. The speeches (and there were many) were potent in burning eloquence and patriotism; the most pleasing part of which (at least to me) was the eulogistic breathed for our favorite Senator. Every speech was a rich, fervent and enthusiastic panegyric of Douglas. . . . the Resolutions cover our ground pretty well. And you may rely upon it that the honest heart of our people are with you in every particular and though we may loose a few Government post masters and place seekers we'll gain thrice their number from the Ranks of the old live Whigs and Republicans. Calhoun, Dougherty, Carpenter, Cook and Leib and many of the paid tribe were here trying to foment difficulty and plot your ruin. With the aid and countenance of a few Black Republicans who sat with them in convention (to prevent their numbers from appearing too ridiculously meager) *they went through the motions*. The Republican organ is to fix out the programme" (James A. Barret to Douglas, April 22, 1858, Douglas Papers, Box 15, folder 41).

10. *Journal*, March 4, 1858. That Lincoln was to be a candidate seemed taken for granted. A report on Lincoln, spinning one of his yarns to make a point on the Kansas fight, was printed in the *Register* on February 25, 1858, from the Peoria *Transcript*, and the following day was reprinted in the *Journal*. Under the heading "The Great Congressional Fight," the story used a blank line instead of Lincoln's name, and referred to him as "a well-known ex-congressman—the one who is to be elected to the U.S. Senate next winter as Douglas' successor . . . of course every man in the crowd desired to know *his* opinion, for he always has an original way of illustrating it." After relating (blank line's) yarn, based on a situation with a client, the *Transcript* concluded, "If there is a better illustration of the result of the memorable conflict in Congress than the case above, we should like to hear of it. In order to be appreciated, however, one should hear [blank line] tell it. No man can 'get off' a thing of the kind with more comical effect." The articles on the reapportionment case were in the *Journal* of February 3, 4, 8, 17, and in the *Register* of January 23, February 4, 8, 9, 1858. In addition, the *Journal* of February 4 and the *Register* of February 5 include Lincoln's name as a member of the Board of Managers of the Illinois State Colonization Society, when announcing a meeting of the society at the First Presbyterian Church on February 8.

11. *Journal*, April 19, 1858, quoting the *Chicago Journal*.

12. *Register*, April 20, 1858.

13. For the *Register's* continuing

attention to Wentworth as the likely candidate or as the one who would spoil Lincoln's chances, see January 4, 28, March 30, April 28, May 21, 27, June 4, 12, 17, 21, 24, July 8, 12, 1858. See also the *Journal* on April 27, 1858.

14. The *Journal* makes mention of Lincoln's campaign prior to the state convention in one way or another, but never extensively, on April 19, 27, May 3, 21, June 3, 10, 11, 14, 15, 1858. Finally on the day of the convention, June 16, the *Journal* addressed the Eastern press under the heading "Illinois Sends Her Answer" and exposed the well springs of Lincoln's approaching nomination. "The conductors of the eastern journals, says the Chicago *Tribune*, who have recommended the Republican party of Illinois to return Mr. Douglas to the United States Senate, as the 'representative of their policy and the exponent of their principles' must by this time, be thoroughly satisfied that, had they attended to their own affairs and refused to meddle with ours, they would have saved themselves the mortification of a defeat. Republican Conventions have just been held in one hundred counties of this State, for choosing delegates to the State Convention, and in ninety-five of them resolutions in favor of Abraham Lincoln, as Mr. Douglas' successor, have been passed, without a single dissenting voice. The unanimity of expression from Chicago and Cairo, alike in counties where Republicans poll three-fourths of the votes, and other counties where Fremont found but two men who dared support him is without parallel in our political history. We assure our eastern contemporaries who have been so sorely troubled with fear that the Republicans of Illinois could not take care of their own affairs, that this action, where not spontaneous, has been provoked by their interference, though it is the result of no arrangement or concert. It is the natural and expected remonstrance against outside intermeddling. It it the answer of Republican Illinois to the managers and wirepullers who would have taken her under their own control. Now let these officious gentlemen help us to repair the mischief that they have done, or hold their peace."

15. The *Journal* sometimes gave Douglas even more attention than the *Register*. When Douglas opposed the English Bill, a compromise measure on the Lecompton Constitution, in a hard-hitting Senate speech, the *Journal* printed the entire speech. Wanting to heal some of the wounds in the Democratic party, the *Register* merely noticed the speech but did not print it. The *Journal* badgered its neighbor until the *Register* relented and gave its readers the speech. Shortly thereafter, Edward Conners, one of the *Register* editors, lost his federal patronage job, another victim of the Buchanan axe. The *Journal* wept crocodile tears for the destructive work it had done in forcing the *Register* to publish a Douglas speech. For this exchange, see the *Journal* of May 18, 20–22, 24, June 8, 1858; and *Register* for May 19, 22, June 9, 1858.

16. The volume of correspondence in the Douglas Papers at the University of Chicago from Illinoisans of all political persuasions approving of Douglas's

stand on Kansas in the period December, 1857, to June, 1858, is impressive evidence of the bipartisan feeling in his favor. Evidence of Republican support even in Springfield comes from Simeon Francis's letter to Douglas, suggesting that Douglas, in the face of the malignant and determined opposition of Buchanan, run for Congress from the Sixth District in place of the ailing Major Harris where he would be assured of election. "Nobly have you stood your ground," wrote the former *Journal* editor. "Though not your political friend, I have been and am your personal friend; and though I cannot feel that I should be doing right in withdrawing my vote for Lincoln as Senator, still would I be glad to do some little for you, to the extent of my ability, to sustain you before the country" (S. Francis to Douglas, May 3, 1858, Douglas Papers, Box 16, folder 21).

17. Republican conventions of Union County, Jackson County, Gallatin County, Christian County, and Johnson County were among those reported in the *Journal* as passing resolutions endorsing Lincoln and praising Douglas, on June 14, 15, 16, 1858.

18. William H. Herndon, *Herndon's Lincoln: The True Story of a Great Life*, 3 vols. (New York, London, Paris: Belford, Clarke & Co., Brentano's, 1889), 2:399–400.

19. Basler, *Collected Works*, 2:461–62.

20. When the *Register*'s ally, the *Chicago Times*, expanded the attack upon Lincoln's Mexican record to include a charge that he had voted against war supplies for United States troops, including the wounded, the *Journal*

responded with outrage at the "most villainous and malicious personal assault upon the Hon. ABRAHAM LINCOLN of this city," and warned that the people of Illinois would resent an attempt "to pull down so honest and high-minded a man and so courteous a politician as Mr. LINCOLN has ever proved himself to be" (*Journal*, June 25, 1858). When Lanphier admitted in the *Register* that its friends at the Chicago *Times* were in error (*Register*, June 26, 1858), editor Shehan was furious. "I knew as well as you did that Henry gave the vote you refer to [opposing military supplies for U.S. troops in Mexico], but Lincoln let the bars down once, & I intend to fasten it on him at the right time. Your article comes right in & lets him escape. Every Republican paper will quote you, & no matter how strongly I prove my case, your denial will have gone forth" (J. W. Shehan to Lanphier, June 28, 1858, Lanphier Papers; Patton, *Glory to God*, vol. 4.

21. *Journal*, June 28, 1858.

22. *Register*, July 2, 1858.

23. Ibid., July 9, 1858.

24. *Journal*, July 12, 1858.

25. Ibid., June 10, 1858, reprinted from the *Chicago Press and Tribune*.

26. *Journal*, July 12, 1858.

27. *Register*, July 19, 1858.

28. Ibid., July 15, 1858.

29. Basler, *Collected Works*, 2:501.

30. *Journal*, July 15, 1858.

31. *Register*, July 19, 1858.

32. Basler, *Collected Works*, 2:508, 509, 518, 519, 520, 521.

33. *Journal*, July 19, 1858.

34. *Register*, July 20, 1858.

35. Ibid., July 23, 1858.

36. Ibid., July 24, 1858.

37. Ibid., July 28, 1858.

38. Ibid., August 7, 1858. In evaluating Lincoln's definition of the

nation's problems, Frederick Douglass remarked that it was "well and wisely said. One system or the other must prevail. Liberty or slavery must become the law of the land. And men, communities, parties, churches and public measures are ranged on one or the other side, favoring the ascendancy of one or the other." The *Register* assumed that the "negro audience spread their gills, rolled their eyes, and clapped their hands with joy that their leader had left their work in such zealous charge as Mr. Abraham Lincoln, black republican candidate for senator in Illinois!" The *Register* explained that such proceedings were the way "the woolly movement works, while in some quarters, and especially hereabouts, Mr. Lincoln's organs attempt, by shallow sophistry to cover up the true designs of his party. It seems, that the negroes themselves, more candid, will not permit this to be done. They insist that their candidates shall 'face the music,' and call things by their right names." Notice of Frederick's speech was sent to Stephen by a friend in Chicago. "You will observe that the 'Black Douglas' places precisely the same construction on Mr. Lincoln's language that you yourself do" (J. R. Vaughn to Douglas, August 5, 1858, Douglas Papers, Box 19, folder 22).

39. *Journal*, August 16, 1858. In an item two days later, the *Journal* quoted another speech by Frederick Douglass alluding "to his pale brother Stephen A.: 'Once I thought he was about to make the name respectable; but now I despair of him, and must do the best I can for it myself.'" The *Register* introduced Frederick Douglass into their columns fre-

quently, just as Stephen Douglas did in his speeches. There is no evidence that Frederick Douglass and Lincoln met prior to August 10, 1863. See Christopher N. Breiseth, "Lincoln and Frederick Douglass: Another Debate," *Journal of the Illinois State Historical Society* 68 (February 1975): 9–26.

40. *Journal*, August 7, 1858. See a later retort by the *Register* to the *Journal*'s repeated use of the *DeKalb Sentinel*, October 1, 1858.

41. *Journal*, August 17, 1858.

42. Douglas to Lanphier, August 15, 1858, Lanphier Papers; Patton, *Glory to God*, vol. 4.

43. Basler, *Collected Works*, 3:5.

44. Ibid., p. 13.

45. Douglas answered Lincoln that regardless of the position of the Supreme Court on the abstract question of whether slavery could or could not go into a territory under the Constitution, "the people have the lawful means to introduce it or exclude it as they please, for the reason that slavery cannot exist a day or an hour anywhere, unless it is supported by local police regulations" (ibid., pp. 43, 45).

46. Ibid., p. 227. The issue over the "Springfield" resolutions figured substantially in the initial meeting at Ottawa, the second meeting at Freeport, and the fifth debate at Galesburg where Lincoln went on the offensive. The resolutions Douglas quoted had been drawn up and adopted in Aurora, Kane County, in the northern part of the state, and were more frankly abolitionist than those apparently adopted by the Springfield Anti-Nebraska or Republican Convention in October, 1854. At all events, Lincoln had escaped signing his name even to the milder species.

by getting out of town. A curious gap in the *Journal's* coverage of the convention in October, 1854, left unchallenged the *Register's* account a few weeks later, which had included the Aurora resolutions as those adopted in Springfield. The editor of the Jacksonville, Illinois, *Morgan Journal*, who had been present at the Springfield convention, charged at the time that the *Register's* account was a forgery. The debate between the *Journal* and *Register* following Douglas's use of the resolutions in Ottawa continued throughout the campaign and took up space by the column foot.

47. The most conspicuous defection was Lincoln's old law partner, John T. Stuart, who authorized the *Register* to state that "ON THE SLAVERY QUESTION HE COINCIDES WITH MR. DOUGLAS—*that he is wholly opposed to the republican party, and* TO ANY FUSION BY WHIGS WITH THEM—that on account of his *personal* relations to Mr. Lincoln, he is unwilling to take any part in the senatorial contest, and shall not vote for representatives to the legislature" (*Register*, October 8, 1858).

48. Ibid., September 25, 1858.

49. *Journal*, October 20, 1858. The *Register's* own final effort to identify Lincoln with Negro equality came on election day when it used block print items throughout its columns, such as the following: "Lincoln says that a Negro is your equal"; "Remember that Lincoln is an abolitionist up North, but opposed to negroes down in Egypt"; "The Union was made for white men, and white men should rule it. To uphold this doctrine vote the democratic ticket" (*Register*, November 2, 1858).

50. *Register*, October 22, 1858.

51. See for example, ibid., October 23, 1858.

52. Ibid., October 27, 1858. Major Harris published an appeal in the *Register* of October 20, 1858, for Douglas's reelection that reasserted the personal dimensions of the contest: "the people of the whole country require them [his services] there, or in a higher position, which it is ordained he soon will reach. His condemnation would be as unjust as has that of Socrates, and it would be followed by a sense of regret and shame an hundred fold greater than was manifested by the Athenians after they had destroyed their greatest philosopher."

53. See for example, *Journal*, October 21, 1858.

54. *Journal*, October 30, 1858.

55. Basler, *Collected Works*, 3:334.

56. *Register*, November 3, 1858.

57. *Journal*, November 8, 1858.

58. Ibid., November 13, 1858.

59. *Register*, November 10, 1858.

60. Ibid., July 26, 1858.

61. On November 13, 1858, the *Journal* reported that the *Sandusky (Ohio) Register* "announces the nomination of Hon. Abraham Lincoln for the next President, by an enthusiastic meeting at Mansfield, in the State." On November 15 the *Journal* quoted an article from the *Chicago Democrat* reporting that "Mr. Lincoln's name has been used by newspapers and public meetings outside of the State in connection with the Presidency and Vice Presidency, so that it is not only in his own State that Honest Old Abe is respected, and his talents and many good qualities appreciated; and through the North and in most of the border States, he is looked upon as an able statesman

and most worthy man, fully competent to any post within the gift of the people of this Union." The *Journal* itself observed on November 10 that "We think Seward and Douglas the two men of the nation least likely to be Presidential candidates in 1860." (In the same issue, the *Journal* quoted the *Rochester* (New York) *Democrat*'s observation that "Mr. Lincoln has won a reputation as a statesman and orator, which eclipses that of Douglas, as the sun does the twinklers of the sky. The speeches made during the Illinois campaign, have been read with great interest throughout the country, and the able, outspoken efforts of the Republican standard bearer, have appeared in very favorable contrast with the subtle sophistry of his plausible adversary. The Republicans of the Union will rejoice to do honor to the distinguished debator of Illinois.")

Chapter 8:
Lincoln and the Constitution

1. Clinton Rossiter, ed., *The Federalist Papers* (New York: New American Library, Mentor Edition, 1961), pp. 290–93 (no. 45), 309–10 (no. 48), 322 (no. 51), 414 (no. 68), 443 (no. 73), 464–66 (no. 78).
2. Carl N. Degler, *Out of Our Past: The Forces That Shaped Modern America* (New York: Harper & Row, 1959), p. 200.
3. Roy P. Basler et al., eds., *The Collected Works of Abraham Lincoln*, 9 vols. (New Brunswick, N.J.: Rutgers University Press, 1953–55), 4:196, 434.
4. Alexander H. Stephens, *A Constitutional View of the Late War Between the States: Its Causes,*

Character, Conduct and Results . . ., 2 vols. (Philadelphia: National Publishing Co.; Chicago: Zeigler, McCurdy & Co., 1868–70), 1:12; William B. Hesseltine, *Lincoln's Plan of Reconstruction*, Confederate Centennial Studies, no. 13 (Tuscaloosa, Ala.: Confederate Publishing Co., 1960), pp. 36–37, 141.
5. "Law Address of Ex-Senator James R. Doolittle, Delivered Before the Union College of Law at Chicago, June 6th, 1879," *Journal of the Illinois State Historical Society* 19 (April–July 1926): 82–83.
6. Basler, *Collected Works*, 3:146.
7. Phillip S. Paludin, *A Covenant with Death: The Constitution, Law, and Equality in the Civil War Era* (Urbana: University of Illinois Press, 1975), p. 15. See also, Harold M. Hyman, *A More Perfect Union: The Impact of the Civil War and Reconstruction on the Constitution*, Civil War Centennial Commission Series, *The Impact of the Civil War* (New York: Alfred A. Knopf, 1973), p. 447.
8. Clinton Rossiter, *The American Presidency* (New York: Harcourt, Brace and Co., 1956), p. 74; Samuel Eliot Morison, *The Oxford History of the American People* (New York: Oxford University Press, 1965), p. 658; James Bryce, *The American Commonwealth*, 2d ed., 2 vols. (London: Macmillan and Co., 1890), 1:289.
9. David Donald, *Lincoln Reconsidered*, 2d ed. (New York: Random House, Vintage Books, 1961), pp. 187–208.
10. Basler, *Collected Works*, 4:430; 7:281.
11. Thomas Jefferson, *The Writings of Thomas Jefferson*, ed. Andrew A. Lipscomb and Albert Ellery Bergh, 20 vols. (Washington, D.C.: Thomas Jefferson Memorial

Association, 1904), 12:418, 183. See also, Arthur M. Schlesinger, Jr., *The Imperial Presidency* (Boston: Houghton Mifflin Co., 1973), pp. 23–25.

12. Carl B. Swisher, *The Taney Period, 1836–1864*, The Oliver Wendell Holmes Devise History of the Supreme Court of the United States, vol. 5 (New York: Macmillan Publishing Co., 1974), pp. 844–50.

13. Rocco J. Tresolini, *Justice and the Supreme Court* (Philadelphia: J. B. Lippincott Co., 1963), p. 16.

14. Frank Otto Gatell, ed., "Roger B. Taney, the Bank of Maryland Rioters, and a Whiff of Grapeshot," *Maryland Historical Magazine* 59 (1964): 263.

15. Bernard Schwartz, *The Reins of Power: A Constitutional History of the United States*, American Century Series (New York: Hill and Wang, 1963), p. 94.

16. Robert H. Jackson, *The Supreme Court in the American System of Government*, The Godkin Lectures at Harvard University (Cambridge: Harvard University Press, 1955), p. 76.

17. Basler, *Collected Works*, 1:112; 4:264.

18. Ibid., 2:400–403, 495; 4:268.

19. Ibid., 8:100.

20. Ibid., p. 52.

21. Ibid., 4:267.

22. Bertrand Russell, "The Future of Democracy," *New Republic* 90, May 5, 1937, p. 381.

Chapter 9:
Lincoln, the Civil War, and the American Mission

1. Roy P. Basler et al., eds., *The Collected Works of Abraham Lincoln*, 9 vols. (New Brunswick, N.J.: Rutgers University Press, 1953–55), 8:332.

2. See Kenneth M. Stampp, *And the War Came: The North and the Secession Crisis, 1860–1861* (Baton Rouge: Louisiana State University Press, 1950), pp. 31–45.

3. The most scholarly statement of the case against Lincoln is Charles W. Ransdell, "Lincoln and Fort Sumter," *Journal of Southern History* 3 (August 1937): 259–88. For a defense of Lincoln, see Richard N. Current, "The Confederates and the First Shot," *Civil War History* 7 (December 1961): 357–69. Lincoln explained in his July 4, 1861, message to Congress: "The Executive . . . having said to them [the seceders] in the inaugural address, 'You can have no conflict without being yourselves the aggressors,' . . . took pains, not only to keep this declaration good, but also to keep the case so free from the power of ingenious sophistry as that the world should not be able to misunderstand it." Basler, *Collected Works*, 4:425.

4. See especially Lincoln to Thurlow Weed, December 17, 1860, Basler, *Collected Works*, 4:154. On the question of evacuating Fort Sumter, see Richard N. Current, *Lincoln and the First Shot* (Philadelphia: J. B. Lippincott Co., 1963), pp. 92–96.

5. Basler, *Collected Works*, 4:259.

6. Allen T. Rice, ed., *Reminiscences of Abraham Lincoln by Distinguished Men of His Time*, (New York: North American Publishing Co., 1886), p. 475.

7. Basler, *Collected Works*, 2:126.

8. See Arturo Uslar Peitri, "Eso que los Europeos Llamaron Nuevo Mundo," *Américas* 28 (April 1976), pp. 9–16.

9. Robert C. Winthrop, *Life and Letters of John Winthrop* (Boston: Ticknor and Fields, 1867), p. 19.

10. John C. Fitzpatrick, ed., *The Writings of George Washington: From the Original Manuscript Sources, 1745–1799*, 39 vols. (Washington, D.C.: Government Printing Office, 1931–44), 26:483–86.

11. Ibid., 35:217–18, 234.

12. Daniel Webster, *The Works of Daniel Webster*, 10th ed., 6 vols. (Boston: Little, Brown and Co., 1855), 5:56, 288.

13. Richard K. Crallé, ed. *The Works of John C. Calhoun*, 6 vols. (New York: D. Appleton and Co., 1851–57), 4:507.

14. Basler, *Collected Works*, 2:130–31.

15. Ibid., p. 266.

16. Lincoln made this statement in his Springfield speech of June 26, 1857, and repeated it in his Alton debate with Douglas, October 15, 1858. Ibid., pp. 405–06; 3:301.

17. Ibid., 2:255. Repeated in 3:14.

18. Ibid., 2:323.

19. Ibid., 1:113; 4:426, 7:23.

20. Ibid., 4:266.

Index